Fish Food

To order additional copies of *Fish Food,* by Rachel Lemons,
call 1-800-765-6955.
Visit us at www.reviewandherald.com for information on other
Review and Herald® products.

Fish Food

What if God values relationship more than religion?

Rachel N. Lemons

REVIEW AND HERALD® PUBLISHING ASSOCIATION
Since 1861 | www.reviewandherald.com

This book was
Edited by William Cleveland
Copyedited by Amy Prindle
Designed by Emily Ford / Review and Herald® Design Center
Cover art by © Thinkstock.com
Typeset: Minion Pro 11/13

PRINTED IN U.S.A.

16 15 14 13 12   5 4 3 2 1

Library of Congress Cataloging-in-Publication Data
Lemons, Rachel, 1983- .
Fish food : what if God values relationship more than religion? / Rachel Lemons.
    p. cm.
1. Spirituality. 2. Bible stories. I. Title.
BV4501.3.L444 2013
220.6–dc23
            2012006428

ISBN 979-0-8280-2539-3

Dedication

I was recently watching a show on PBS called *Royal Family*, which explained royal British life. On this particular episode Prince Charles was scheduled to visit a family-owned organic farm where the owners would host him for tea.

The owner's wife had a quaint tea set decorated with cute, cartoony farm animals. While this set was a typical household item, the husband thought it would be best if the dishes that were used when the prince sat at their table were gilded and glitzy.

I waited as time progressed in the show to see who would win this particular battle—the husband or the wife. With the magic of TV, within minutes I watched the prince sit at the couple's table; the camera panned on the small kettle and the four teacups and saucers. The front of each dish boasted a cutesy animal, with a large spotted cow on the kettle.

When the host purchased the set, I'm sure she never imagined they would be used to serve the prince of England. I often feel that way—like a common, unworthy vessel, chipped at the edges, not quite fit to play the part. Please know that I write this book more to myself than to anyone else, because if anyone is a sinner, I certainly am.

Before all else, I would like to praise God for the learning experiences He has brought me through in order to be able to put pen to page. I feel more honored and loved than I could have ever imagined possible. I would like to dedicate this book to my mom, dad, Pernell, Tim, Brent, Mrs. Horton, and anyone else who had the task of reading or hearing about *Fish Food*.

Contents

Introduction

God is a God of relationships, and most of us can appreciate that. Over the course of our lifetimes we've probably had several BFFs: (best friends forever). My first best friend, whose title was understood but never declared, spanned kindergarten. The next best friend was a bit more forward in declaring our friendship. We were in third grade, and I was the new kid in class. Some of the other kids didn't like me right away because they said I thought of myself as cool (and I was).

One day while preparing to go home, I was in the hallway gathering my coat and book bag. Along came one of the girls with whom I carpooled, and she saw me talking with a cute Asian boy with black, pin-straight hair and wire-framed glasses. She immediately put her hands on her hips and demanded that I tell her who he was. Before I could say his name, he boldly announced that we were best friends. I stood there a bit befuddled, but eventually shot back with some smart remark. Since that moment he was "green frog" and I was "pink flamingo." The thought of it still makes me smile. Though time and life have pulled us apart, I still love him like we're back in third grade. My next few BFFs had relationship lengths of a few years, and I still think of them all fondly.

My current best friend was my third roommate in my first year of college (long story—don't ask). We bonded over Billy Holiday and cracking jokes about the deans and RAs. Oh, the inside jokes!

I'm sure that someone exists in your life with whom you have your own inside jokes. Whether your next-door neighbor growing up or your high school chemistry lab partner, to you that person is like no other. How did you develop that friendship? We all know that time can make or break a relationship. When we spend time together, our bonds are typically strengthened, and when we spend time apart, our bonds can be weakened.

While my BFF and I have had many special memories, one really sticks out in my mind—as much for what I did as for what I didn't do. To set the scene: it was our first year of college—no cars, little money, no Valentine's Day plans. She decided we would have Valentine's Day dinner anyway, so she dug out a plug-in skillet and started making a festive entrée. I, on the other hand, went to my office job, happily knowing that after my shift I would enjoy a Valentine's Day meal.

On my way back from work I felt as if my stomach were eating itself. I was so hungry that I felt as if my body was taking on the type of weightlessness seen only in cartoons, causing it to float down the hall in sync with the smell of food.

What happened the minute I walked into the room is still a point of contention. I blame it on my hunger. I opened the door, and my eyes immediately locked on the food; I felt as if it were drawing me in. In a very cavewoman-like way, I jammed my fork into the skillet and broke off a large section of the veggie meat that sat in a delicious labor-of-love sauce, all while my BFF wasn't looking. I must have chewed especially loud, because after a few bites she whirled around and screamed in protest, "Noooo! No! Stop!"

I shrugged it off, thinking she was acting like an overzealous chef, striving for a certain measure of perfection while I was fine with "good enough." As I continued to chomp on her creation, I looked at her in confusion.

"You ruined it!" she exclaimed.

"Ruined what?" I asked, unfazed between bites.

She let out a frustrated sigh. "The heart—you ruined the heart!"

I stopped midchew and thought of spitting it out, as though that would restore its shape. Instead I gave a hard swallow. Guiltily I looked back in the skillet and saw the remnants of the heart shape.

She looked miffed. And though I praised her profusely for the rest of the heart-shaped meal, I could tell it wasn't the same. I was satisfied with "good enough" while she created perfection. And this is the dilemma in our relationship with God. God tirelessly tries to give us perfection, but we tend to be impatient and think we're satisfied with "good enough." Or maybe when it comes to our relationship with God, we think we're satisfied with nothing at all.

I wrote this book out of great urgency. I asked God so many questions about who He is and what He is like that in response, He gave me this nagging sensation to write a book called *Fish Food* that addressed my many questions. As you'll learn over the course of the book, the title describes an experience. It's a time in your life that might seemingly work to your detriment and appear to take you out, but God uses it for your good.

No matter your religious affiliation or where you are on the relationship spectrum with God, as you read this book I want you to ponder three questions: When was the time you felt the closest to God? When was the time you felt the furthest away? What were the circumstances in your life that brought you to those places? Knowing these answers will put you in the perfect place for relationship building with God, which is the purpose of this book.

I understand we all come from different places, different denominations, and different levels of faith and maturity in our relationship with God. Some of us have no faith at all, but somehow we ultimately want the same thing. We want God to show up, and be real and apparent. When hardship and destruction come, we want clarity and a solution. We want to see a manifestation of God. We want to know that our God is as real as our pain.

We often blame God for the things that happen in our lives. We tend to think He is watching in the midst of crisis in mocking silence, waiting to taunt, "I told you so." It's always easiest to blame the person who's not (physically) in the room. That way they can't talk back. But how many times have we had the boldness to shake our fists at the sky and dare God to show Himself? Would we be surprised if He appeared before us? If He answered matter-of-factly, "Yes, how may I help you?" Maybe we don't really want Him to appear, because if we did, wouldn't we seek Him a little harder? He promises in Jeremiah 29:13, "You will seek me and find me when you seek for me with all your heart."

Perhaps you are reading this book out of curiosity, or because someone gave it to you. Maybe you're reading it as an assignment. However you found yourself with this book in your hands, know that by reading it you will find yourself on the same journey on which I have found myself.

In this book I have opened myself to you in a very vulnerable way in an effort to show you how God longs to be in a relationship with you. He is a God of relationship before He is a God of religion. No matter where you are on the relationship spectrum, know that when you acknowledge to God where *you* are, He can pick you up and take you where He wants you to be.

Remember Who You Are and Whose You Are

Living With Purpose:
The Story of Jonah

Growing up, I always wanted a pet: a cat, a dog or even a hamster. Whatever it was, I wanted it to be cuddly and furry. However, my mom had a different concept in mind. She opted for caged, furless, well-restrained pets (as in birds and fish).

My first pet parakeet died an untimely death when he ran into the side of the cage. My second was given to a church member after I mysteriously developed a bout of allergies toward the bird. But while I had these birds, they were entertaining companions. The fish, on the other hand, I found to be rather unexciting. There was one thrill, however, in having fish as pets: feeding time. It was the one real interaction I could have with them. I enjoyed watching as the fish vacuumed up their meal bit by bit.

As humans, we have a fascination with animal feedings. If you doubt this statement, just watch Animal Planet. Viewers sit in gross anticipation as a hapless antelope strays too far from the herd, only to meet its demise as a lion pounces upon it. We watch not for the scenery but rather for the interspersed bouts of feeding. Perhaps this explains the draw of the story of Jonah. It's the ultimate animal feeding experience, in which one of God's spokespeople morphs into "fish food." Or maybe what really attracts us to this story is that we realize, more times than we'd like to admit, that we are a lot like Jonah with our own "fish food" experiences.

Jonah ran from God. He didn't jog or walk quickly; he booked it! When God told him his task, he took the first ship out of town.

While the task was not completely comfortable, it was the job God had given him. God has told us, "I already know the plans I have for you. I will help you, not hurt you. I will give you a future and a hope. You will call on me and I will answer. You will talk to me and I will listen. You will seek me and find me as you search for me with all your heart" (Jeremiah 29:11-13, Clear Word).

In this case His plan for Jonah was to go to Nineveh. Imagine if God chose you to go to Las Vegas, Chicago, or Miami to convince the inhabitants of their sins. Would you go? Would you own the task God had given you? Perhaps we don't literally run, as Jonah did, but we may avoid the calling, ignore the urges, or shut out the still small voice. We must remember who we are and whose we are, which translates into learning to live with purpose.

God has called each of us in two ways: He has called us to *be* someone unique and to *do* something specific. For this reason He uses specific situations, tailor-made for us, to speak to us. For me it has always been through different cultures. God knows my love for various languages and cultures, so He has always used them to get to my heart.

Although I attended a Christian college, I did not have a striking spiritual experience while I was there. Not because it wasn't a spiritual place, but because it simply didn't move me—perhaps because the spirituality felt so familiar. I thought I'd heard it all before. However, the summer before my senior year I decided to study in Brazil to learn Portuguese and experience Brazilian culture. I met Christian young people who were very sincere in their friendships and in their faith. Sometimes during prayers to bless the food I would crack my eyes open just to witness the sincerity etched on the students' faces. They were truly grateful for the food that sat before them, and they were grateful for the opportunity to talk to their God. I could both see it and feel it. It was the smallest thing, yet it moved me. Never before had I witnessed such a large group of Christian young people who were so sincere about their faith. I realized that God had spoken to me in my language—through another culture.

When God speaks to you, it's as though the mechanic who dreamed up the concept for your new car, sketched it out, created the model, searched for the parts, wielded the tools, and then wrote the owner's manual comes by your house to replace the bulb when the right headlight goes out. He understands the intricacy and inner workings of the creation because He conceptualized it, designed it, and put it together. David explains it in this way: "You shaped me before I was born; you put my bones together while I was still in my mother's womb" (Psalm 139:13, Clear Word). So if you share your spiritual experience with someone and they don't quite get it, or their enthusiasm doesn't match yours, don't be discouraged. It was *your* experience, tailor-made for you.

So Jonah ran. But more surprising than the run was his reason for running. Jonah ran and bought a ticket on a cargo ship in an attempt to get away from God. However, God had no intention of leaving Jonah. As soon as the ship took off, the winds blew, shaking the boat fiercely and rattling the sailors.

The Bible almost seems to fast-forward through the action. What happens in these three verses of the Bible would give filmmakers fodder for a 45-minute scene, building the drama and suspense, setting the action to music to further engage the emotions of the viewer. However, in Jonah 1:3-6 the action unfolds without pause: "[Jonah] went down to Joppa, where he found a ship bound for that port. After paying the fare, he went aboard . . . to flee from the Lord.

"Then the Lord sent a great wind on the sea, and such a violent storm arose that the ship threatened to break up. All the sailors were afraid and each cried out to his own god. And they threw the cargo into the sea to lighten the ship.

"But Jonah had gone below deck, where he lay down and fell into a deep sleep. The captain went to him and said, 'How can you sleep? Get up and call on your god! Maybe he will take notice of us, and we will not perish.'"

Have you ever taken a cruise? Picture this: As you walk along with your towel tossed over your shoulder, preparing to go to the pool on deck, a storm indiscriminately turns the sky above you a moody shade of gray. The wind begins to whip sheets of water onto the boat, threatening to sweep everyone on deck overboard. As the waves crest, the ship sits on the edge of a wall of water, in danger of spilling into the dark valley below. The crew employs all of its emergency maneuvers. The jokes at the beginning of the trip that lightheartedly suggested a second *Titanic* become a looming reality. As the ship begins to take on more water, the crew suggests that some of the heavier items be tossed overboard to release some of the stress being placed on the ship. At first, crew members strategically choose items of which to dispose. An hour later, after the storm has shown no sign of letting up, items that were previously deemed to be essential to a prolonged survival are now being tossed. A sense of panic, topped with the most basic human desire to survive, is thick in the air. The crew has grown desperate and begins to plead with everyone around them to pray to their gods, whoever they might be. At this time there is no discrimination—they all grasp for faith in something or someone, as long as it means a chance for survival.

This was the feeling aboard that cargo ship headed to Tarshish. Desperation had set in. All aboard feared for their lives. During the time of Jonah there was no hope of sending a Mayday message to the Coast Guard or hoping a wandering helicopter would spot the troubled vessel. In the case of an overturned ship, the crew and all of the cargo were sure to be lost.

In the midst of the chaotic religious rituals, someone noticed that while everyone else on the ship was on the deck pounding their chests, ripping their clothes, chanting, and rocking, one man was not among them—that Jonah guy. The one who arrived right before the ship prepared to take off and who continuously glanced nervously over his shoulder as if someone were following closely behind him.

The captain paused between his recitations and scurried below deck in search of the missing passenger. It wasn't long before he found Jonah curled up in the corner, unaware of what was transpiring above him. The captain shook him to full consciousness. The urgency in his voice signaled to Jonah that he must rush to deck immediately. Upon his arrival, a chaotic scene greeted him.

On the backdrop of the most ferocious storm he had ever seen was a cacophony of chants, prayers, recitations and supplications. As his eyes wandered over the men aboard, each appeared more devout and sincere than the one before him. Immediately a sinking feeling came over Jonah as he realized that this dramatic scene, set to the crackling of thunder and accented by flashes of lightning, was for him. The men begged him to pray to his God, thinking that perhaps *He* was the God of the wind and the rain.

When the storm continued to rage on, the men decided to cast lots; the lot fell on Jonah, and then the inquisition began. Why was this happening? What had he done? Jonah answered the men without hesitation: He had run away from his God. Finally the men had someone to blame. He was the cause of the torrent of rain and the whips of wind that threatened to crack the ship in half. The men demanded that Jonah tell them what to do to calm the storm. Jonah stated simply, "I must be thrown overboard."

This went against the code. The sailors always strived to keep everyone on the ship alive, and they were uncomfortable with this idea. But they were also anxious to survive. After asking Jonah's God for pardon in advance, they reluctantly threw Jonah overboard. Immediately a calm came over the water, wind, and rain. The power of Jonah's God spoke to the men aboard the ship, and that day they promised to make Jonah's God their God.

For the men aboard the ship, the story ended there. But for Jonah the journey had just begun. Typically when we hear the story of Jonah, the terrible part of the story is that Jonah was literally swallowed by a "huge fish"

(Jonah 1:17). God could have allowed Jonah to have the same supernatural buoyancy He allowed for Peter when he walked on water; however, God allowed Jonah to sink. The waves washed over him, and I imagine he felt as if he were drowning. Jonah shares the sensations he experienced as he recounts his journey into the depths of the ocean: "I sank into the sea like a person falling into a pit. I went down past the base of earth's mountains. There was no escape" (Jonah 2:6, Clear Word).

A quick evaluation shows us that the sinking and the near death experiences were really terrible. But getting swallowed by the big fish was actually what *saved* Jonah's life. "But Lord, you saved me through this great fish. You heard my prayer and brought me up from the deep" (verse 6, Clear Word).

Situations like this, which appear dismal and unsolvable, are designed to perfect us and bring us closer to God. In fact, we can see these situations as our "fish-food" experiences. In life we must all endure them—it's how we deal with them that distinguishes our characters.

Jonah was not the only biblical character who was given a specific and daunting task to do, but he was the only one, recorded in the Bible, who literally ran away with such determination. God had very precise undertakings for biblical characters to carry out, and each one reacted differently. Moses was called, and he stuttered. Saul was called, and he was blinded. Esther was called, and she fasted and prayed. Samuel was called, and he responded readily. Jesus was called, and He died. Jonah was called, and he ran! But even in Jonah's hasty escape attempt, there are many things we can stand to learn.

Just as He called Jonah, God has called us to be someone unique and *do* something specific. For this reason He gives us experiences that are tailor-made for us, designed to expose our flaws so He can rework them. After we learn our purpose we must stand up, claim it, and own it. We may become overwhelmed at the gargantuan size of the task or by our minuscule abilities to complete it. As a result, we will oftentimes run away, just as Jonah did. But through our God-assisted ability to endure our fish-food experience, we will grow—and people around us that we least expect may grow as well.

Throughout the rest of this book we will explore how God has called each of us to be someone unique and do something specific. Each chapter will explore an aspect of relationship building and restoration with Jesus. The principles are presented against the backdrop of familiar biblical characters. As you read, pray that God opens your eyes so that you may either get to know Him for the first time or learn to appreciate Him and your relationship with Him in a new way.

Looking in the Mirror—What Do You See?

How Do You View Your Faith?
The Story of Daniel, Shadrach, Meshach, and Abednego

was once asked if I had ever questioned my faith. The question made me stop and quickly reflect on how I view myself in comparison to the rest of the world. So now I pose that question to you. Do *you* ever question *your* faith (or the lack thereof)?

The person who asked me was a good friend with a different religious background. He was deeply curious if I simply ascribed to my religious beliefs because of my upbringing, or because I had truly pondered, kicked the tires and done a thorough inspection.

I responded, "All the time." I elaborated and said that as a Seventh-day Adventist young adult I probably had to question my faith more than young adults of many other religious backgrounds, because oftentimes I was different from those around me. What about you? Do you blend into the world, or are you noticeably different?

What is different? One morning, while doing my hair, I got the novel idea that I would 'fro my hair out—1970s love, peace, and hair grease style. So I got a blow dryer with a comb attachment and a pick and went to work. I picked and picked, patted and patted, until finally I had created a round ball of wonder that sat like a halo around my head. However, when I walked out of the house, I got even more attention than I had bargained for—at the post office, in class, on the streets. Everybody I ran into somehow had some memory or feeling associated with *my* Afro.

Is that how God calls us to be different? Is it merely in our appearance? While we can distinguish ourselves outwardly, it's even more important for us to differentiate ourselves on the inside. We need to exhibit beautiful characters that stand out. Characters equivalent to a lime-green mohawk or to my Afro that cause people to stare, because they rarely or never see anything like it. We're talking about characters that reflect the character of Christ.

There were various young people in the Bible who were unafraid to stand out from the crowd and exhibit distinctive characters. Those who first come to my mind as having had the fiercest experience in this area are Daniel and his three friends, Hananiah, Mishael, and Azariah—better known by their Babylonian names, Shadrach, Meshach, and Abednego. Individuality, uniqueness, and independent thinking did not scare them, because they knew who they were and whose they were.

Although they were young when they were captured, they were firmly embedded in their faith. This strong understanding gave them assurance and confidence in their decisions, as they knew and believed in the reasons they did or did not do certain things. It made them unafraid to stand out from the crowd. In fact, there were three distinct occasions during which either Daniel or his friends had to deviate from the crowd and stand by a decision that made them different from those around them. We will explore two of those experiences in this chapter.

The first we find in Daniel 1, which tells of the battle between Jehoiakim, king of Judah, and Nebuchadnezzar, king of Babylon. After God allowed Nebuchadnezzar's army to win the battle, Nebuchadnezzar took with him the spoils of war. These things that he carried away were not only for the purposes of increasing his wealth, but also to allow him to have bragging rights. It's one thing for a burglar to enter your house and steal your TV, leather jacket, and camera; it's quite another for the thief to take all those things in addition to your handsome, intelligent son as a captive—a prisoner of war, a slave.

That's exactly what Nebuchadnezzar did. Not only did he steal the articles from the Temple—he also had Ashpenaz, chief of his court officials, capture some of the young, healthy, and very intelligent Israelite men from the royal family and nobility. Imagine how that played out in Judah. The sacred Temple had been defiled, and royal families were stripped of their prized possessions—their sons.

But King Nebuchadnezzar did not have slave labor in mind for these young, intelligent lads. Such prized captures were set to do a higher work: They would serve in the king's court. During this time King Nebuchadnezzar ruled over a large portion of the world, and he needed a lot of advisers to help him run the show. First, however, these advisers needed to become educated. And in order for them to be able to concentrate fully, they needed to eat the best food possible. So the king provided the perfect setup. He arranged for the young men to receive a proper Babylonian education over the course of three years, while eating the same foods he ate.

Imagine the first time the food was served to the young Hebrew boys. Many probably salivated at the thought of getting to try this rich, foreign, and exotic food. This was their first time away from home, and although it was sad to be away from their families, they weren't being treated poorly. Eating the same food as the most powerful king in the world couldn't be so bad. It was a little different from what their mothers would have prepared, but there was little they could do.

But as Daniel and his three friends saw the food being served to the others at the table, there was a sinking feeling deep inside that said to them that they could not do as everyone else was doing. Daniel 1:8 tells us that Daniel decided, even though his name had been changed to Belteshazzar (which means "Bel protect the king's life"), that he would represent his God. And in this case that meant not eating food from the king's table.

In this situation we see that even before Daniel was faced with the external confrontation, he internally made his decision. All too often we make decisions for the benefit of others. We do things to maintain appearances. We make decisions in the moment, often depending on our mood or outside influences. As a result, the decisions we make are not consistent with what we say we believe. From this situation with Daniel we learn that we must first be consistent with ourselves before we can show consistency in our behavior toward others.

Daniel approached Ashpenaz and explained the situation. Working in the king's court, Ashpenaz probably thought he had heard it all before—but never had he heard a request like this. Of all the captives, he had four guys who did *not* want to eat the same food as king. As much as Ashpenaz respected and had grown fond of Daniel, he couldn't honor that request. If the king found out he was responsible for the "malnourishment" of the boys with water and vegetables, he would surely lose his head. They were serious about punishment in those days.

But Daniel did not take no for an answer when it came to decisions that would compromise his beliefs. He understood why he did what he did. Although he was out of his family's house for the first time and could have gone willy-nilly, he understood the reasons behind his beliefs. And Daniel 1:9 tells us that because Daniel stood firm for God, God worked on his behalf.

When Ashpenaz said no, Daniel asked Melzar, the personal tutor assigned to him and his three friends, to test them for 10 days. Daniel 1:12, 13 says, "Please test your servants for ten days: Give us nothing but vegetables to eat and water to drink. Then compare our appearance with that of the young men who eat the royal food, and treat your servants in accordance with what you see." So Melzar agreed, and after 10 days (to his surprise, I'm sure) the young men looked stronger and healthier than any of the others on the king's diet.

The second time I think of in which Daniel and his three friends stood out from the crowd is found in Daniel 3. Here we find Daniel's friends in a sticky situation. Sometime after Daniel interpreted the king's dream, something in the king's attitude began to shift. At the time of the interpretation Nebuchadnezzar was awed at the abilities of Daniel's God. He was floored at His power, and as a result he paid respect to Him. But time passed, and Nebuchadnezzar began to mull over the large, statuesque image in his mind. And after contemplation, he somehow reasoned that he could manipulate the meaning of the dream. His kingdom would *not* pass away, and he would show proof of that by building a statue of pure gold to show that his kingdom would last forever. In order to solidify his power, he would make those around him honor him by bowing down to the statue. Those who refused would be thrown into a fiery furnace.

On the inauguration of the image the crowd was thick with executives, bureaucrats, and chief advisers. Nebuchadnezzar likely held a sort of trickle-down theory: If he could get the leaders on board, the masses would surely follow. And in order to create a more conducive environment for worshipping the image, he provided atmospheric music. The order was that once the music began playing, all in attendance should show their respect by bowing down.

The first chord was struck, and immediately, probably similar to "the wave" at a ball game, the sea of people threw themselves down to the ground. The king looked over his loyal subjects smugly and was quite pleased with his revised version of history. His kingdom would surely stand. At the end of the chorus of instruments serving as a sound track for his musings of a kingdom that would last forever, he was interrupted by several of his Chaldean advisers. A bit perturbed by the intrusion, he demanded to know what was so important as to take precedence over his thoughts of continued world domination.

The Chaldeans reported that there were rebels among them. Three Jewish young men had not bowed down during the chorus of music. Nebuchadnezzer's anger brewed at this blatant disobedience, especially in the face of such a momentous occasion. He demanded that the three be brought before him. When his advisers said their names, he realized he knew these men; they had never been a problem to him in the past, but this type of defiance was *definitely* a problem. As he contemplated how to handle the situation, he concluded that he would provide the young men with another opportunity. Perhaps they didn't understand the command, or maybe he could play some music that was more to their liking. If the problem was their Hebrew God, perhaps his orchestra could play a riff of one of their Jewish hymns to put the young men at ease.

As Nebuchadnezzar saw the young men arrive, he demanded a reason for such defiance in front of the entire kingdom. He explained with a good dose of anger, as though talking down to naughty children, that he would play the anthem again, and this time they were to bow! No questions asked. He would not tolerate insubordination two times in a row. The second act of defiance would be rewarded with the fiery furnace. That would teach these rabble-rousers.

With deeply honest and humble voices, the young men expressed that there was no need for Nebuchadnezzar to strike up the band a second time. They were assured in their decision. And if God decided to deliver them from the fiery furnace, so be it, but if He did not, then that was His decision. Either way, they could not compromise their beliefs.

This threw King Nebuchadnezzar over the edge. Even as he attempted to be merciful, the young men had dealt his ego a sizable blow by declaring that they would not obey him. At this point they left him with no other decision than to make good on his word. He ordered the furnace to be made hotter, to match the wrath that burned within him. The young men were bound as if they were common criminals. The guards led the three to the furnace, inched toward the entrance, and threw the trio in. The sheer force of heat that emanated from the giant bonfire killed Nebuchadnezzar's guards.

The king eased back into his portable throne. A bit of his rage eased away as he stared at the mesmerizing flames. The king blinked twice to adjust his vision. Apparently the waves of extreme heat were causing him to see what he was seeing. His hand claimed a death grip on the guard standing next to him. With shock and awe he asked, "How many men do you see in the furnace?"

The king continued: "We threw three men in the furnace, bound hand and foot, and four walk freely in the flames. The fourth man looks like a son of the gods! Call them to come out!"

The air was thick with amazement as the young men emerged from the flames. The other officials, who had come from all around the kingdom for the momentous occasion, gathered around and touched the men's hair and clothes to confirm what they had just witnessed. Just as it appeared, neither a hair nor a thread of the men's clothing had been burned. On that day, although King Nebuchadnezzar had planned to declare his kingdom as lasting forever, he declared that the kingdom of Shadrach, Meshach, and Abednego's God would never fall.

As we have seen in these instances, standing out requires taking action. Not only must you set your purpose in your mind and in your heart—you must also convince your body. It's not enough to believe your beliefs; you must live them as well. However, it's not always easy to take action. Especially if you don't know the person on whose behalf you are acting. You must know Jesus before you can confidently and appropriately act for Him. And that is what we will explore in the chapters to come: relationship restoration, building and how to take action in our lives as Christians.

Falling in Love With Jesus

Relationship With God:
The Story of the
Samaritan Woman at the Well

When he walked into the room, the world seemed to lurch to a sudden slow-motion speed that's possible only in chick flicks and action movies. Though we were only in high school, he already had a swagger about him. His casual laugh signaled that he didn't have a care in the world. I glanced shyly over at him, intrigued and smitten by his apparent good looks. Then suddenly it hit me—that nagging sensation that I had to know more about this guy.

That same feeling about Jesus didn't hit me until I was a young adult. We had brief encounters in the past: a gentle brush by one another as we crossed paths, a short conversation before dinner, a small exchange during church or before a big test. But we had never had a deep, intimate interaction. I had never let Him take an in-depth look at my faults and flaws and analyze the reasons I did the unseemly things I did. Because those areas weren't so attractive, I thought I'd keep them aside until He fell for me (little did I know how much He had already fallen). "But God demonstrates his own love for us in this: While we were still sinners, Christ died for us" (Romans 5:8).

So what was the difference at this time in my life? Had He changed, or had I?

And then I found my answer in the most unlikely place. One summer, in the wasteland of reality shows intended to replace well-plotted TV dramas, a well-known network proudly boasted a new show designed to turn modestly shy men into the ultimate "pick-up artist"—a man apt at making women swoon upon his entrance and skilled at winning their affections. Each week the audience watched in amazement as the men soon developed a cocky air about them that seemed to draw women in. They had mastered the art of getting a woman to return their affections. After six weeks on the show, the *men's* interest in getting to know women better remained unchanged. The only difference was that now the *women* were responding in a new way.

There it was. Thanks to that show, I was struck with the realization that Jesus hadn't changed and neither had His love. The difference was that *I* had never reciprocated His show of affection in a way that led Him to believe I was interested.

"Behold, I stand at the door and knock. If anyone hears My voice and opens the door, I will come in to him and dine with him, and he with Me" (Revelation 3:20, NKJV).

To be honest, at this time what really led me to reciprocate His earlier attempts to get to know me was the pain of a hard breakup. I guess you could say Jesus was my rebound guy, only this relationship would turn out to be no short fling. Typical of a rebound, I spilled my guts to Him about the last relationship. I contemplated the reasons it didn't work out. I recounted the good times and the heartaches. He listened without interrupting. He consoled me. And finally, when He saw I had said my last piece, He prompted me to open His Word and take comfort in His promises. Knowing how much I like to see the puzzle pieces fit together, He spoke to me in my language of logic. He showed me through Scripture that if earthly parents know how to give good gifts to their children, just imagine the types of gifts He knows how to give to His children.

"Which of you fathers, if your son asks for a fish, will give him a snake instead? Or if he asks for an egg, will give him a scorpion? If you then, though you are evil, know how to give good gifts to your children, how much more will your Father in heaven give the Holy Spirit to those who ask him!" (Luke 11:11-13).

You are My daughter, He said to me.

"See what great love the Father has lavished on us, that we should be called children of God! And that is what we are!" (1 John 3:1).

He kept speaking to me. *Therefore, if the gift isn't good and perfect, it isn't from Me. And when it is good, you'll know it's from Me.*

"Every good and perfect gift is from above, coming down from the Father of the heavenly lights, who does not change like shifting shadows" (James 1:17).

As I heard this, I got excited. What girl doesn't like to receive gifts! The more I got to know Him and experience His personality and character, the more I wanted to know. I had to understand and know this Man they said was like no other. Little did I know that "Rebound Guy" was turning into something much, much more.

As I later read the story of the Samaritan woman, I imagine that she had similar hopes. She must have expected that her rebound guy would turn into something more. In fact, five times she had hoped and five times she had been disappointed—until that day when she met Jesus at the well.

When I read this story in John 4:1-30, I feel as though I am watching a romantic comedy about a woman searching for love amid a series of failed relationships. Over the course of time you watch as this fairly attractive woman bounces from relationship to relationship, each time trying to fill the void within her. Although the first marriage doesn't work out, you seem to understand why, given the circumstances. The couple, quite young when they met, rushed into things. The foundation of the relationship wasn't strong, and eventually things gave way until there was nothing left. The woman, broken and quite unsure of herself, walked away.

As you watch the story unfold on the screen, it's apparent that the woman is quite vulnerable and perhaps should take a break from relationships, surround herself with friends and family, find a useful hobby, develop herself and invest in her relationship with God. And with the wisdom of a silent observer on the other side of the screen, you wince as she accepts the attention of an ill-intentioned man who offers to carry her moving boxes from the house of her ex-husband. This small show of affection is just the attention she craves to temporarily bandage the wound her previous marriage has inflicted. She soon moves into a small apartment across town and is visited frequently by her surprisingly available knight in shining armor. All too soon, neatly placed little bandages quickly hide the wounds of her first marriage, and within six months she's betrothed to her (new) beloved. Though her mother, aunts, and host of female cousins frown in disapproval when they receive the (new) set of wedding invitations in the mail, they manage syrupy-sweet smiles while in her presence. While helping with the arrangements (the second time around) they mutter little comments to each other, but never within her earshot. Soon enough she's married and moved in with the love of her life (for the second time). With a sinking feeling her parents say a quick prayer outside of her new home, hoping things will finally work out.

As the movie progresses, the director gives obvious signs foreshadowing imminent doom. The cheerful wedding ditty that once set the stage for the characters' joy is now replaced by the ominous chorus of stringed instruments. The camera pans on the couple's house as their initial marital hopes of happiness, lovemaking, shared meals, and annual vacations have given way to good old-fashioned bickering and bitterness. And as improper as it seems, they decide it's best to cut things off early, so as not to prolong the obvious tension and disappointment. If it isn't working, it isn't going to work.

On several additional occasions we the audience allow our hopes to be raised and dashed as she wanders from one broken marriage to the next—each time duped into believing that this time would be different from the last. To be honest, the fourth husband, a professional from a good family, shows promise, for he is willing to overlook her flaws (and they are many). However, after so many broken relationships, she just doesn't know how to reciprocate his show of affection.

On this day, when the downtrodden character prepares to make her way to the well to fetch some water for the house she shares with her live-in companion, we long for her to experience a supernatural streak of good fortune. So we are more than thrilled when she happens upon Him that day at the well.

She gently lowers her bucket until she hears the reassuring splash it makes when hitting the water below. She allows the water to fill the bucket, and a tiny smile pulls at the edges of her lips as she recounts the stories her mother has told her about the history of this deep recess of water. Jacob, his sons, and all their livestock drank from this very same well. The thought of it is reassuring, but as she realizes how far she has wandered from her childhood self, the smile quickly erases from her lips. She begins to retrieve her bucket from the darkened hole when a gentle voice interrupts her thoughts.

"Will you give me a drink?" (John 4:7).

She looks around, first to see who is speaking and second to make sure He's speaking to her. But as she suspects, just the two of them stand at this famed well. *What are his intentions? What does he want from me?* Men didn't often talk to her just to see how she was doing. Though she has been duped many times in the past, she knows this time she will proceed with caution. She will be the one asking the questions.

"How is it that You, being a Jew, asks a drink from me, a Samaritan woman?" (verse 9, NKJV).

This question will surely reveal his intentions. Immediately, without mincing words, Jesus goes to the heart of the matter.

"If you knew the gift of God and who it is that asks you for a drink, you would have asked him and he would have given you living water" (verse 10).

What an unexpected answer! Her mind immediately wanders back to her mother's words about this well. It once belonged to Jacob and his sons. *Is this man somehow greater than he?* The question nags within her mind. *And where is his bucket? How does he intend to draw water from the well?* As much as she tries to contain herself, she can't. Propriety has never constrained her before. She replies, "Sir, you have nothing to draw with and the well is deep. Where can you get this living water? Are you greater than our father Jacob, who gave us the well and drank from it himself, as did also his sons and his livestock?" (verses 11, 12).

Jesus, always open to questions, replies, "whoever drinks the water I give them will never thirst" (verse 14).

Either this man has supernatural abilities or a very clever marketing technique. I'm not sure where this water is coming from, but it sounds like something I have to have.

"Sir, give me this water so that I won't get thirsty and have to keep coming here to draw water" (verse 15).

And then, allowing the conversation to take an unexpected turn, Jesus responds by asking her to bring her husband. This twist to the conversation can be defined as the most poignant moment of the story. How does a simple request for water turn into a serious inquisition? The Samaritan woman is definitely taken aback, but being familiar with sticky situations such as this, she sticks to the truth.

"I have no husband," she replies flatly (verse 17).

Jesus says to her, "You are right when you say you have no husband. The fact is, you have had five husbands, and the man you now have is not your husband. What you have just said is quite true" (verses 17, 18).

At that moment she experiences a sinking feeling, similar to the one her parents felt when they dropped her off at a new husband's house. *How does he know such things about me? Could he be a prophet? If so, what is his angle?* Determined to get to the bottom of this, she poses the following: "Sir, I can see that you are a prophet. Our ancestors worshiped on this mountain, but you Jews claim that the place where we must worship is in Jerusalem" (verses 19, 20).

Jesus adeptly responds with absolute clarity, "Woman, believe Me, the hour is coming when you will neither on this mountain, nor in Jerusalem, worship the Father. You worship what you do not know; we know what we worship, for salvation is of the Jews. But the hour is coming, and now is, when the true worshipers will worship the Father in spirit and truth; for the Father is seeking such to worship Him. God is Spirit, and those who worship Him must worship in spirit and truth" (John 4:21-24, NKJV).

The Samaritan woman's heartbeat begins to quicken. *Could it be?* She poses the question, hoping to learn a bit more about this insightful Man who stands before her.

"'I know that Messiah is coming' (who is called Christ). 'When He comes, He will tell us all things'" (verse 25, NKJV).

Jesus responds clearly, "I who speak to you am He" (verse 26, NKJV).

Just as it hit me in my young adult life, it hit the Samaritan woman that day at the well—that nagging sensation that she had to know more about Jesus. What's particularly striking in this story is the Samaritan woman's desire to get to know Jesus. As she fires off question after question, it's obvious that she's curious to know more. Despite all of her previous relationships, the Samaritan woman now had the perfect attitude for relationship building. In her questioning of Jesus she had finally reciprocated His show of affection, and the Bible says in Jeremiah 29:13, "You will seek me and find me when you seek me with all your heart."

This nagging sensation to know more is often born out of need. In John 4 Jesus skillfully uses the human needs of thirst and hunger to explain our spiritual need of Him. Even during the story of the Samaritan woman at the well, Jesus first opens her eyes to her need of Him by using something so simple—water. After she realizes her need, Jesus deals with her issues, which are apparent through numerous failed attempts at relationships. Finally He teaches her how to have a relationship with Him, through worship. In the end she is so compelled by this experience that she goes off to tell anyone who will listen.

"For Christ's love compels us" (2 Corinthians 5:14).

I find it interesting that the Samaritan woman, who was ready to build a relationship with Jesus, was found at a well. There's something significant about wells in the Bible: Many of them mark the location for life-changing experiences.

Sometimes a well was used as a type of boot camp or training ground. Take Joseph, with his coat of many colors. God was able to use this harrowing experience of Joseph being thrown into a pit to shape his life in an extraordinary way. At other times He's used them as a meeting place. Isaac's wife, Rebekah, was found at a well when Abraham sent his oldest servant on a special search mission. The well played a significant role in the answer to his servant's prayer (Genesis 24). But most significant is that in all cases, the well signifies a source of blessing, either as a result of the characters' experiences there or through the literal sign of God's blessing, as was the case with Isaac (Genesis 26:15-22).

While the well itself is important for its ability to sustain life, it's useless if you don't drink from it. The same is true in our relationship with God. It's insufficient to have a one-time moving experience with God. He longs to have a relationship with you, and relationships require continual care and nurture. Yes, you must oftentimes be rescued. But then you must learn how to live. You must learn to push through the hard times and hold on tightly to God when He says "No" or "Wait," or even when He is silent. But the only way you'll build this type of relationship is by learning to talk with God on a regular basis.

Praying Like There's No Tomorrow

Learning How to Pray:
The Story of Samuel

Coming to God With Open Hands

I am learning to pray with open hands—open to letting go, open to giving and open to receiving. I do this because most often, when I approach God with clenched fists instead of open hands, the object of my prayer is usually somewhat self-serving. And frequently in these instances, God says no to my prayer requests, which causes me to think of Him as being stingy and unwilling to say yes. However, I am learning that when I come to God with open hands, *He* doesn't change, but our relationship does. Although I still approach Him with my desires, my hands are open to His answer, knowing that He has even more of a vested interest than I do in seeing that I get what is best for me (James 1:17). Therefore I am willing to let go of the request if necessary, give if He asks me to, and receive whatever He deems sufficient.

Let me explain further. Imagine it is your child's bedtime and you must collect the toy he is playing with and get him ready for bed. Is it easier to take the toy when the child's hands are clenched tightly or when the child's hands are open? Now imagine that you must take the toy from him while at church, during the sermon, or at the grocery store. The shouting that is likely to ensue from the child with the clenched fists will surely make you look like a tyrant. Well, that's how we make God appear when we approach Him with closed hands. We present our request with clenched fists and throw a fit when He attempts to take something from us or when His answer is "No" or "Wait." However, in this approach to prayer, we cheat ourselves, because not only do closed hands refuse to let go, they also cannot receive. So lately I've taken to praying with open hands, allowing me to be more receptive to God's answers. But I had to learn this lesson the hard way.

I don't believe I truly learned to pray until I was in my early 20s. Prior to that I went to church, Sabbath school, and Christian schools all my life, but I didn't learn to really pray in those environments. Just as we don't appear to need a doctor until we're sick, similarly we sometimes don't think we need to pray until we're in the midst of a difficult situation. My prayers were born out of a dark cloud of sorrow. When you're in deep pain, you need an equally strong painkiller—and that's what prayer became for me.

"The Experience"

He left me breathless . . . and not in the romantic way. After almost nine years he left me breathless in a way that sucked the life out of me. He left me feeling as useless as a glove with no hand to fill it. The fabric of our relationship started to unravel like a loose string hanging from the hem of a shirt. One strong tug, and the whole thing began to come undone. One evening, after leaving work late, I saw what I thought was my boyfriend's number on my phone, and I smiled in anticipation at listening to his message. I dialed into my voice mail, my ears prepared to hear the gentle lilt of his voice. What greeted me instead was the strong intonation of a confidently misguided young woman. Within the first few words of her message she boldly identified herself as *my* boyfriend's girlfriend.

I know it all sounds complicated, and it was. At that very moment a burst of adrenaline shot into my blood, causing my heart to go into overdrive. Every sense in my body was awakened. Simultaneously my nose flared, my eyes stung, my fingertips tingled, my tongue pricked, and my ears rang. I immediately began to dial everyone in my inner circle, and miraculously, no one answered the phone. I was unsure how seven girls were all unavailable at one time. I tried my best friend once more, but still no response. At this moment I virtually collapsed into the arms of God. For once in my life I had no idea what to do or how to deal with the situation. My mind raced. What would I say? How would I react?

The inevitable conversation with my boyfriend occurred later that evening, and after a series of questions that could have carried the title of The Great Inquisition, the truth spilled from the mouth of the accused. At times he was stammering, defensive, offensive, and flabbergasted. When the conversation finally ended (though not for lack of things to talk about), we hung up the phone. I paced the open space in my bedroom. I was numb and expressionless. The man with whom I had shared almost nine years of my life had committed the ultimate betrayal. Every ounce of my life that I had previously weighed out to be reality was turning out to be a weightless sham.

I glanced around the room, looking for something to throw. A primal scream was caught in my throat. I was too overcome with pain to let it loose. Finally I collapsed in the middle of my bedroom in a helpless ball and wailed. I cried because the future would not be what I had always dreamed. I cried for the children we would never have together and the in-laws I would never meet. I cried for the loss of my invested time, love, and energy. I cried because I couldn't understand how good could be rewarded with evil. I cried at the blatant show of selfishness and self-indulgence. But mostly I cried because I just didn't know what was next. And that's when my first prayer was born. Though I'm not sure how many of the words I cried were intelligible, I am sure that God understood every one of them.

Prayer Defined

Prayer. It's such a loaded word that carries power and hope, but also mystery and silence. We know that through it God has given us a way to talk to Him personally; it's the replacement for being able to carry on face-to-face conversations with Him as the first family once did in the Garden of Eden. Prayer is the lifeblood of our Christian experience, and without it, living a Christian life is impossible.

However, we often think of prayer as a particular act during a moment in time. We pray before we drive our cars. We pray before meals. We pray before a big test, when someone falls ill, or when we need to make a big decision. But I would like to suggest that prayer is an experience. How else can we "pray without ceasing" (1 Thessalonians 5:17, NKJV)?

It took me a while to understand this concept. There was a time in my life I had a looming prayer request that felt like my shadow, as it was with me at all times. During this period of my life I thought praying was like placing an order for fries. The ticket was sitting back in the kitchen, but I hadn't gotten my food yet. I continuously brought the request before God. I journaled the prayer, I fasted and prayed; I even brought two or three together to gather in God's name, and although I saw small progress, I never noticed any significant change as a result of my prayer. Eventually my focus on my prayer request began to wear me down, causing me to have pent-up frustration toward God. I became so focused on the request that I hardly paid attention to the Grantor of the request.

In the midst of being miffed, I shared my feelings with a friend who I knew had a strong relationship with God.* I made a few snide comments about how God was ignoring me. I told him that I felt like the "forgotten" child. I lamented my situation, and I made sure everyone knew about it. He listened, and after much silence he made a suggestion that revolutionized my spiritual life: "Have you ever tried spending time with God without asking Him for anything?"

Well, what's the point of that? I thought to myself. That's like sitting on Santa Claus's knee, as a kid, and not asking for a present. His words stung for a while, partly because I wanted to feel as if he didn't know what he was talking about. However, something about his words eventually rang true for me.

As simple as it sounded, I had never done it before. Even when my first prayer was born, it was done out of pain. I was crying out for God to reconcile my relationship and to deliver me from the pain I was experiencing. However, I was not approaching God with a real desire to spend time with Him. *He* wasn't the object of my affection; His ability to heal me and give me what I wanted was the real object.

So now that I had tried everything else, I decided just to spend time with God as a friend. As we discussed in chapter 3, I was finally in the perfect place for relationship building. As I spent time basking in who God is, my attitude toward Him shifted. And this led me to the understanding that prayer is so much more than an act—it is an experience. In this way we are able to experience prayer without ceasing, because prayer is all about seeking God. That's what is meant by Matthew 6:33: "But seek first his kingdom and his righteousness, and all these things will be given to you as well."

The primary objective is God's kingdom. Therefore, the objective of prayer is to seek (and find) God. Everything else is captured in "all these things." They are the secondary objective.

But what is seeking God all about? Is it like playing a game of Marco Polo with Him? This is often how I felt in my prayer life, simply yelling "Marco!" and blindly groping toward God as He cleverly ducked and dodged to avoid my grasp.

Most often I felt like this when I was in the middle of making a big decision. In times like these it seemed as though God moved the slowest. But when I saw prayer as a mere act, it was natural for me to expect a quick, one-time reply from God. However, now that I understand that prayer is an ongoing experience, it makes sense that the answer to prayer is often a process and a learning experience. For instance, we ask God for a bike and expect to get a brand-new red Schwinn at our doorstep. Instead he sends a box of bike parts along with a how-to manual for putting it together.

Although it requires a shift in thinking to regard prayer as an experience instead of just an act, it does come with a guarantee. Continuously throughout the Bible God promises that we will find Him when we open ourselves to finding Him. "You will seek me and find me *when* you seek me with all your heart" (Jeremiah 29:13).

That is an awesome promise, and there are similar promises sprinkled throughout the Bible. Our God is one who assures that He will show up when you open yourself to having a relationship with Him and hear what He has to say. If you ever forget it, visit the following verses for a reminder. Hebrews 11:6; James 1:5; Proverbs 3:5, 6; Psalm 105:4; Isaiah 55:6; James 4:8; Jeremiah 29:13; Deuteronomy 4:29; Lamentations 3:25; Matthew 6:33; 2 Chronicles 15:2; Acts 17:27; Proverbs 8:17; Matthew 7:7, 8.

It's similar to the concept we looked at in the beginning of the chapter about approaching God with open hands. We cannot receive a relationship with God when we have tightfisted hands. Imagine trying to hold hands with someone whose hand is clenched. While it's possible, it certainly doesn't make you feel welcome. This is similar to our relationship with God. We must seek Him or present to Him a hand that is open and willing to hold on to His hand.

But even with the knowledge that prayer is an experience and that we must approach God with open hands, this still leaves unanswered questions, such as How do you pray? and Does prayer really work? There are two ways I encourage you to answer these questions for yourself. First, review the prayer lives of others. Consider this part of your prayer experience to be test prep, like studying for a final exam or career field entrance exam. You don't know exactly what will be on the test, but you can learn test-taking strategies.

If you haven't noticed by now, life is a series of tests and emergency situations that are overcome only through prayer—and lots of it! Studying how those in the Bible prayed their way through life's challenges is like pulling out the Kaplan software or going to the LSAT prep course. We're able to study their strategies and learn how to approach God in prayer. I've often found it helpful to understand how those before me have had successful prayer experiences. I've wondered how they approached God, how often they prayed, how they felt, and how God responded. We can stand to learn a lot by observing how God has moved in the past. Here's your first round of review for the test:

- Samuel told the Lord to speak to him, and He did (1 Samuel 3:10).
- Daniel was faithful in the times that he prayed (Daniel 6:10).
- Enoch prayed to God as he would speak to a friend (Genesis 5:22-24).
- Hannah poured out her heart to God (1 Samuel 1:10).
- The widow in the parable in Luke 18:1-8 was persistent.
- David recognized his need for forgiveness and repented (Psalm 51).
- Jacob struggled with God and knew where his blessing came from (Genesis 32:26).
- Job showed his emotion to God, but did not curse Him (Job 1:18-22).
- Jonah prayed for deliverance (Jonah 2).
- Adam told God of his need for a spouse (Genesis 2:20, 21).
- Daniel asked God to show him the future (Daniel 10).
- The disciples asked God to be taught how to pray (Luke 11:1).
- Esther recognized her need to pray with others (Esther 4:16; Ellen G. White, *Prophets and Kings,* p. 601).

Did some of them surprise you? I would encourage you to pick up your Bible and read the stories mentioned above. Through them you will be encouraged in your own prayer life, and they will encourage you to try God for yourself. They can give you the boost you need to develop your own prayer experience.

Before embarking on your prayer journey, remember that it's very important to have faith. As a child, I always heard this concept of having faith, so in an effort to exercise that faith I often asked for things in prayer, having faith that I would receive them. But again, my focus was on my prayer request and not on my God. Over time I've learned that God is the central focus of my faith.

"And without faith it is impossible to please God, because anyone who comes to him must believe that he exists and that he rewards those who earnestly seek him" (Hebrews 11:6). Therefore, as you exercise your faith, make sure it is based on God, and not on your request.

Now let's look at the book of 1 Samuel. There are six lessons in the first few chapters of this book that can be applied to your prayer experience.

Hannah's Distress

I have noticed something amazing about the story of Hannah, especially when told in a continuous line with the story of her son Samuel. We often tell the stories as stand-alones, and while each one is powerful by itself, telling them together helps us to connect the dots between Hannah and Samuel's prayer lives. And most important, looking at their prayer experiences teaches us a lot about ourselves and our own prayer lives.

In 1 Samuel 1 we find a very distressed Hannah. Not only does she have a rival, but the woman who taunts her day and night lives in her house and sleeps with her man. Her name is Peninnah, and she is literally "the other woman"—her husband Elkanah's other wife. The source of her pride is her children, but not because they know their alphabet and numbers. She's simply proud that she was able to *have* them for her husband. While having children seems so commonplace nowadays, during this time giving a husband children (especially boys) was like wearing a badge of honor. Perhaps Peninnah took it over the top because she knew Elkanah loved Hannah more than he loved her, and this was her way of recapturing a bit of affection. For whatever reason, it seemed to boost Peninnah's sagging self-confidence to hit Hannah where it hurt: her inability to get pregnant.

Each year the family would journey to Shiloh to worship and sacrifice, and each year Peninnah would find occasion to make jabs at Hannah. This time, after putting up with Peninnah's snide remarks, which she somehow managed to make syrupy sweet in the presence of Elkanah, Hannah slipped away until she found herself in the tabernacle. As she arrived, she virtually collapsed into the arms of God. She longed for Him to hold her and wipe the tears from her cheeks as her father had routinely done for her as a child. As she rocked with a steady rhythm, her lips moved, but no sound came out. She was so totally submerged in her prayer that she didn't notice Eli, the high priest, approach.

This is where Hannah and God finally met. Now, I'm sure this wasn't the first time Hannah took her request before God, but for some reason He reached out and granted an answer to Hannah in response to her prayer of distress that day. That's our first lesson in prayer.

Principle 1: God Often Reaches Us in Our Distress. Distress Breeds Prayer.
"In my distress I called to the Lord; I cried to my God for help. From his temple he heard my voice; my cry came before him, into his ears" (Psalm 18:6).

There's something about distress that can provide a favorable condition for relationship building, and often this is where God finds and reaches us. I'm sure God would like to reach us in a place other than our distress, but it seems to be in these moments that we are best able to perceive our need of Him and to open our hands to a relationship with Him. Both Samson (Judges 16:21-31) and Saul (Acts 9:1-19) had to experience blindness in order to be open to seeing God. And I see now that it has been in some of my darkest moments that God has been best able to reach me.

While acknowledging that distress is a place God often reaches us, I would encourage you not to wait until you reach your darkest moment to start a conversation with God. Not that I am promising the moment of distress won't ever come if you develop your prayer life, but it will be a lot easier to get through if you know God before then.

Principle 2: Prayer Breeds Answers and Confirmation.

"Then you will call, and the Lord will answer; you will cry for help, and he will say: Here am I" (Isaiah 58:9).

Hannah must have been a sight to see, because when Eli looked over at her he was sure she had wandered into the tabernacle after having a strong drink . . . or two. *How inappropriate*, he thought to himself. *At least she could keep her drunkenness out of the tabernacle.* So, like any good priest, he went over to reprimand her for her lack of respect.

Upon hearing his words, Hannah shook her head, thinking, *You don't know the meaning of these tears. This one is for the sons I cannot bear my husband. This one is for the condescending way Peninnah speaks to me. Each tear tells the story of my sorrow.* But she simply sighed and explained to Eli that she wasn't drunk; she was crying and praying out of overwhelming sadness. Eli then understood, and with compassion he said, "May God answer your request."

This statement was Hannah's confirmation of the answer to her prayer. And shortly after, Hannah became pregnant.

Life is all about redemption. Primarily it's about the redemption Jesus provides us from the sinful lives we lead, but along the way God gives us small moments of redemption as well. Perhaps for you, life is about redemption from a hurtful childhood or from the poor treatment of others. For some it is about redemption from unhealthy relationships and unfair situations. For Hannah, she received redemption from her barrenness.

In this situation we see that God answered Hannah's prayer. In addition, He provided her with a confirmation to the answer to her prayer. Oftentimes in the Bible we see situations in which a person receives confirmation of their answer to prayer after they have been praying about something. For example, in the story of John the Baptist's conception, we see Gabriel come to Zechariah and tell him, "Do not be afraid, Zechariah; your prayer has been heard. Your wife Elizabeth will bear you a son, and you are to call him John" (Luke 1:13). At this time Elizabeth had not yet given birth to John the Baptist, but Zechariah was given a confirmation of the answer to prayer.

God can use whatever He wants to confirm the answer to prayer. When necessary, He has even put words in the mouth of a donkey (Numbers 22:28). In the case of Zechariah, Gabriel proved his credentials in being able to confirm the answer to prayer by saying, "I am Gabriel. I stand in the presence of God, and I have been sent to speak to you and to tell you this good news" (Luke 1:19).

With Hannah we see that she was not pregnant at the time Eli confirmed the answer to her prayer, but hearing this word from a man that was in touch with God was an assurance of her answer to prayer. It was not until later, after an encounter with Elkanah, that Hannah actually became pregnant. So remember as you pray that God may provide us with confirmation of an answer to prayer prior to the prayer actually being answered.

After receiving what she had long asked for, Hannah was grateful beyond measure, so she promised God that she would dedicate her son's life to Him. After Samuel had been weaned, she sent him to Eli so he could help in the tabernacle.

Principle 3: God Calls Your Name.

"The Lord came and stood there, calling as at the other times, 'Samuel! Samuel!'" (1 Samuel 3:10).

Samuel was very helpful around the tabernacle as Eli fulfilled the duties required to keep things in order. One night while falling asleep, Samuel heard a voice calling his name. He quickly jumped up and headed toward Eli's quarters. Perhaps he was thirsty and needed a bit of water.

With quick footsteps Samuel arrived in front of Eli's mat. "Yes, sir. You called?" Samuel asked with childlike humility and respect. Eli groggily turned toward the voice. His eyes took a moment to adjust to the darkness.

"No, child, I did not call you. You may go lie back down."

Samuel shook his head to himself. He knew he heard someone call his name. It was unmistakable. But he crawled back onto his mat and found a comfortable position. As his mind began to wander off to sleep, he heard the voice again.

"Samuel, Samuel!"

He sat up with a start. He looked left and right. Nothing. He got up quickly and ran to Eli's quarters again. This time Eli fixed his eyes firmly on Samuel, wondering what could be going on. *Was the boy feeling OK?*

Similarly, Samuel replayed the sound of the voice in his mind. He was sure he had heard someone call his name. It was undeniable. But Eli sent him back to bed, hoping to be able to quickly fall back asleep.

A third time, after only a few moments of lying back down, Samuel heard the voice again.

"Samuel!"

A third time Samuel ran to Eli's room. Samuel was sure he had heard his name, and Eli wasn't one to play tricks. This time Eli was wide awake. He sat up and looked directly at Samuel. Though it was rare these days for God to communicate directly with people, Eli was familiar with stories of men in the past receiving a call from God in this way. So Eli told Samuel that if he heard the voice again, he should answer, "Speak, Lord, for your servant is listening" (verse 9).

Principle 4: Learn to Recognize His Voice.

"My sheep listen to my voice; I know them, and they follow me" (John 10:27).

We often think that God does not speak out loud to people in modern days. The reality may be that people in modern days have so much noise in their lives that they don't know how to discern the voice of God. I have often found that God must repeat Himself to me. When I hear Him the first time, I write the voice off as being my "self-talk"—therefore I tend to disregard the importance of what I hear. When God really needs to get something across to me, I usually make Him say it twice. The key is learning to recognize God's voice so that He needs to speak only once before the message is heard and followed right away.

When Samuel lay down again that night, he heard the voice of God call his name a fourth time. This time Samuel recognized the voice and immediately responded, "Speak, for your servant is listening" (1 Samuel 3:10). What an amazing moment!

Principle 5: Share Your Experience With Others.

"Then the word of the Lord came to Jonah a second time: 'Go to the great city of Nineveh and proclaim to it the message I give you'" (Jonah 3:1, 2).

When God speaks your name and has a specific message for you, it is like no other experience in the world. It is a one-of-a-kind call with a heavy-duty responsibility attached. Remember, God didn't wake Samuel with good news. He told him that He was about to judge Eli and his family, because Eli had let his sons, Hophni and Phinehas, run the tabernacle like a casino without ever correcting their behavior. So God gave Samuel the heavy news that He was going to remove Eli's family from their priestly office. I'm sure that young Samuel must have felt burdened with the message God gave him. It's also likely that Eli suspected something because in the morning he was anxious to ask Samuel what God had to say. With honesty, Samuel shared the message God had given him. With humble acceptance Eli said, "He is the Lord; let him do what is good in his eyes" (1 Samuel 3:18).

Principle 6: Engage in an Ongoing Conversation With God.

"Enoch walked faithfully with God; then he was no more, because God took him away" (Genesis 5:24).

What's amazing about the story of Samuel is the ongoing conversation he develops with God from the first moment He calls him by name. When we imagine prayer, we often think of sending requests to God. In the story of Samuel we can observe that prayer is not a monologue but a conversation.

A review of 1 Samuel 8 lets us examine the situation when the children of Israel asked for a king. Samuel was hurt by this request, but he brought it before God. We see in verse 6 that Samuel prayed about this request, and in the following verse God answered him, saying that the people had rejected *Him* and not Samuel, and that Samuel should indeed give the people a king. However, it's not just in this moment that we see a dialogue between God and Samuel. Throughout the first 15 chapters of 1 Samuel, we see that Samuel would pray and God would answer. God would give Samuel a message, and he would share it. It was this continuous conversation that framed Samuel's relationship with God.

How can you practice these same principles in your life? How can you learn to recognize the voice of God and unfold an ongoing conversation with Him?

Personal Prayer Experience

Not long ago, as I began to approach my house on my way home from work, I saw an orangish glow in the distance. It looked as though a nearby house was festively illuminated with Christmas lights . . . in the middle of August. As I rolled to the stop sign I realized the home's garage was on fire. My eyes searched frantically for fire trucks, ambulances, or police cars. There were none. Meanwhile the flames ate away at the structure of the garage without a single pair of watching eyes. With great urgency I floored the gas pedal until I arrived at my house. I threw myself out of the car and very clumsily rushed to the door. I frantically tried to get the key to fit in the keyhole, my hands shaking the whole time. After I finally entered, I floundered through the house, screaming that the neighbor's garage was aflame. I rushed to call 9-1-1. *Ring . . . ring . . .* it felt like an eternity between each sound, then finally an answer.

"A fire!" I screamed. "At 17th and Randolph!"

"Yes," the attendant responded. "We have someone en route."

I hung up the phone and went to my observation point (living room window), taking inventory of the scene: still ablaze; still no emergency response vehicles. The flames from the garage threatened to swallow the nearby house. Each second seemed to stretch into an hour. After at least 10 minutes the fire trucks arrived and set up a theatrical stage. They scurried into motion like windup toys, each one going about their duties. Within minutes the flames were out. Crisis averted. It was obvious they had fought fires before.

How much are our life situations like these fires? We're amazed and overwhelmed. We've never seen such a fire before, so we call on God. He says He has already responded. Help is on the way. But we don't hear the sirens. We don't believe it. All we see are the flames continuing to burn, threatening everything we've built. How could He possibly be on His way? However, when He arrives, He's adept. It's obvious He's fought fires before. The flames are out in a jiffy.

Unfortunately, we treat God like a firefighter or a piece of equipment set aside for extraordinary events. "Break glass in case of emergency." What does that say about how you regard God? What type of friend would you be if you invited someone over only when there's work to be done? How would you feel if the situation was reversed? Moving day—you get a call. Flood—you're on speed dial.

Perhaps this is why we feel as if our cries for help to God have gone unheard. Perhaps we've spent too much time asking and not enough time listening. Perhaps we've skipped the most important aspect of prayer: relationship building.

In chapter 3 of this book we discussed relationship building and maintenance as related to God. Prayer is a natural extension of this relationship. I crave prayer because it means personal attention. Imagine being one of 7 billion children and still getting your Father's ear. I need prayer because it provides satisfaction. It's the feeling of consistency that every long-distance relationship needs. Prayer puts emergencies into perspective. It's the on-time response to the 9-1-1 call.

I don't have a special prayer technique to teach you in this chapter. There's no special prayer rug or prayer beads to use. I won't teach you a string of words to memorize. I can only tell you to go spiritually naked and vulnerable, just as you are, and pour out your heart to your Creator. As you go through your prayer experience, you will have lots of questions. Does prayer make sense? Does God really hear you when you pray? How can you learn to pray within God's will? These questions will begin to create a dialogue between you and God.

Oftentimes we overanalyze prayer. But it won't make sense in the manner of a scientific formula. Unfortunately the supernatural has been so sensationalized on TV and in movies that believing in such things as good and evil as active forces is thought of as being unrealistic. What if the widowed woman had thought "rationally"? She would have never had her miracle meal. If the leper had doubted, he would have remained marred by illness. Had Jairus lacked faith, he would have missed out on the best years of his daughter's life. Prayer requires stepping out on a limb.

As we discussed earlier, faith is often understood to be faith in the prayer coming true. But that is actually more like a wish than a prayer. True faith is fully believing in the God to whom we pray. (Hebrews 11:6).

As a kid, I was in love with stories—so much that I often begged to hear them over and over. Some of the anecdotes from my dad's childhood sounded so incredible to me. My father grew up in rural Alabama in a sharecropper family that picked cotton. Like many families during that period, my father's family was rather large, with six girls and five boys. My father is the middle child, or, as he likes to say, the forgotten child. Perhaps his "forgotten" status stems from one experience in particular. During the time he was too young to go to the field, he was left alone at the house. Although he was just a small child, he sensed that he was by himself, and he began to cry; however, there was no one to console him. After his incessant wails and tears he would become hoarse, having never received the attention he craved.

Many of us imagine prayer to be this way. We think we are one of 7 billion children vying for the personal attention of our heavenly Father. How could He possibly have the time or patience to listen to all of our self-centered requests? But as we look over the prayer lives of those in the Bible, we see that God is faithful in hearing and answering prayers. As I share with you my personal prayer below, I also pray that you will take that first step of faith and approach God with spiritual nakedness and vulnerability and pour your heart out to Him.

God,

I come before You now, wanting to be more like You—but I don't know how. I want to be intimate with You, but I fail each time. When others look at me, I want them to see You. I want to unabashedly expose to You my faults and flaws. I want to stop trying and start doing. I want to stop patting myself on the back for my good efforts that result in failed attempts. You alone are holy and worthy to be praised. I want to know You. I want to love You. I want to know how to love You. I want to see Your face in every homeless man and woman I encounter. I want to know joy. I want to be awed and amazed when I'm in Your presence. I want to trust You totally and completely. I want to wear a smile that speaks to others of our intimate interactions. I want to be more like You. I want to know and experience Your love so intensely that I am compelled to pass it on. God, I want You, but I don't know how to be intimate with You in a lasting way. I'm ready for You to show me how to love.

Amen.

I pray that you will begin your prayer experience with God today.

"I waited patiently for the Lord to help me, and he turned to me and heard my cry. He lifted me out of the pit of despair, out of the mud and the mire. He set my feet on solid ground and steadied me as I walked along. He has given me a new song to sing, a hymn of praise to our God. Many will see what he has done and be amazed. They will put their trust in the Lord" (Psalm 40:1-3, NLT).

---

*Note: Be careful with whom you share your spiritual failings, as you want to be encouraged out of your spiritual slump, not pushed further into it.

When You Don't Have Something Nice to Say ... Praise Anyway

Learning How to Praise:
The Story of Job

Is praise like a progress report? Is it our evaluation of how God is doing? Do we dole it out when He does a good job and withhold it when we're displeased? Of all the topics covered in this book, praise was among the hardest for me to understand, and it has always been a mystery to me. I imagine praise being spoken in a British accent, accompanied by a bow and a curtsy, seemingly saved for kings and princes in fairy tales and said with words that seldom grace the mouths of modern men ("Your Majesty; My Lady; Your Eminence; My Lord"). But what I'm learning is that while these words were designed to put distance between ruler and subjects, words of true praise are designed to bring us *closer* to God and to usher us into His presence.

I've always imagined praise as giving God a compliment. In day-to-day life I usually give compliments only when something extraordinary happens—not for everyday occurrences. I tell people when I like their clothes or acknowledge when they do something especially well. And to read in the Bible that God *asks* for our praise seems to go against cultural norms of feigned humility. Think Goliath in the story of David and Goliath, or Muhammad Ali before his fight with Joe Frazier. Is that how we picture God? Do we revere and respect Him because He walks around with His chest poked out, strutting throughout the universe with manly swagger?

This thought process alone showed me I was in desperate need of giving God praise. Yes, you read correctly: in need of *giving*. Praise is necessary for the restoration of our relationship with God. Our God gauge is off, and praise is the proper way to realign it. Through it we are better able to understand who God is, and this understanding puts us in the perfect place for relationship building.

When Adam and Eve sinned, they failed to take God at His word because they thought they had stumbled upon a better way. And by thinking they knew more than God, they didn't acknowledge who He is. However, they didn't change reality by not acknowledging Him. For example, if you stop acknowledging the existence of gravity, will you begin to float above the earth? Even without acknowledging it, you still experience its effects. The same is true with God, and that's why praise is key. Praise puts us in touch with reality, thereby helping us acknowledge who God is.

We often make the mistake of confusing praise with compliments. We compliment people for what they do; we praise God for who He is. The things God does are supporting evidence of who He is, but there is so much more to Him than what we witness Him doing.

There are several verses I love to read that have helped my understanding of who God is. Whenever I get angry and wonder why God isn't working things out, I visit Job 38-41. Somehow God's strong words to Job always seem to resonate with me as He asks Job to explain the inner workings of the earth to Him. I always feel like a silent observer watching as God asks Job question after question, to which Job could not possibly have a legitimate answer. Then somehow, in the middle of the conversation, I feel as if God stops talking to Job and turns to starts talking to me. Job's silence is then replaced by my silence. And being silent in God's presence puts me in the perfect place for relationship restoration because it is then that I am best able to understand God's depth, breadth, and power.

Whenever I wonder if God is fully in control, I visit Matthew 8. Here the disciples are in a boat with Jesus, who's calmly at rest, when a storm brews in the sea and begins to threaten the men's safety. All the while, Jesus remains asleep until the disciples awaken Him with fear in their eyes. Jesus calmly looks the storm square in the face and commands it to calm down. He actually says, "Peace, be still" (Mark 4:39, KJV). The disciples stare on in amazement and say in wonder, "What kind of man is this? Even the winds and the waves obey him!" (Matthew 8:27).

These are just two verses that really pop out at me and begin to reveal the character of God. You may have some of your own. This is the first step in praising God—being put in touch with reality and understanding who He is.

I loved going to school in the South, because it was so common for men to be courteous. They would trip over themselves to open doors for you, help you down stairs, and help carry things. After being there, I was thoroughly convinced that chivalry was not dead. Call me old-fashioned, but I still appreciate when men allow me to exit the elevator first or open doors for me. As much as some women may disagree with me, I believe it is the man's role to pursue in a relationship and the woman's role to be pursued receptively. In my mind there is something to be said for people playing their roles.

Now, I do realize that sometimes those roles can shift out of necessity. For instance, when I was growing up, my mom typically arrived home at 6:00 in the evening, while my dad arrived at 3:00 in the afternoon. So he would typically cook during the week, and my mom would cook on weekends.

Although roles in our society are shifting in some ways, some roles remain bedrock, including those within our relationship with God. We each have a part to play. As much as He is our buddy and our friend, He is still our God. He's all-powerful, sovereign, all-knowing, and everywhere at once. Isaiah 40:6-8 explains our existence in comparison to God by saying, "All people are like grass, and all their faithfulness is like the flowers of the field. The grass withers and the flowers fall, because the breath of the Lord blows on them. Surely the people are grass. The grass withers and the flowers fall, but the word of our God endures forever."

Do you doubt it? Then answer the question posed in Matthew 6:27: "Can any one of you by worrying add a single hour to your life?"

Praise helps us put ourselves in perspective. After we understand the reality of who God is, we are able to see who we are in comparison to Him, and how pointless it is to obsess or worry.

When was the last time you took a ride in an airplane? Do you remember the sensation you felt as the plane began to take off? After the initial force pushed you back in your seat, you likely glanced out the window to see the objects that once loomed ahead appear as small as Monopoly pieces. When we look at our lives without putting them into perspective, everything we do and own appears so important. However, when we begin to compare them with who God is, they all begin to appear as small and as worthless as Monopoly pieces. Praise not only teaches us who God is—it also helps us understand our role as we put God into perspective.

In second grade the boys in my class got a kick out of making fun of my last name. Admit it, there's a lot you can do with the last name "Lemons." So for the longest time I would think about how I couldn't wait to get married so I could change my name! Mind you, I was about 7, so marriage was a long way off. It wasn't until later that I learned to love my name because it told the story of who I am. Within that name lies generations of people who carried it before me. Have you ever thought about how praise teaches us our names? I would suggest that it is not until we learn who God is that we learn who we are in relation to Him.

"See what a great love the Father has lavished on us, that we should be called children of God! And that is what we are! The reason the world does not know us is that it did not know him. Dear friends, now we are children of God, and what we will be has not yet been made known. But we know that when Christ appears, we shall be like him, for we shall see him as he is" (1 John 3:1, 2). Therefore, by praising God, we are acknowledging the reality of who He is. And when we have accepted Him, we are then learning our names and acknowledging who we are: children of God.

Even as I write about praise I must admit that it is still a journey for me to understand its place in our relationship. Perhaps it's because while growing up, I heard certain praise words so often that I filed them away as Christian clichés. I didn't understand them; they seemed like overglorified flattery and empty words that didn't carry much weight for me personally. So not long ago, when I discovered that praise was vital to the growth of my relationship with God, it dawned on me that I really did not know how to praise Him.

My prayers always began with a quick "thanks for waking me up" and ended with "in your name we pray." In between I managed to sandwich a few requests and then quickly went about my daily activities. Finally, one day in prayer, I admitted to God that I didn't know *how* to praise Him. In fact, I was so bewildered by the concept that I had to look the words up in a dictionary. I tried to excuse myself by saying we live in an honorless society. *Perhaps if I lived in a country with a king,* I thought, *it would be much easier to understand honor, praise, and worship.* But after acknowledging to God where I was, He showed me that He longed to take me where I needed to be, and my first prayer of praise (which I recorded in my journal) went like this:

Dear God,

I've never really prayed a prayer of praise and worship to You. I'm sure Your angels do it all the time. They're always in Your presence and really have a sense of Your mighty power and worth, Your wisdom and Your sacrifice. I don't want to just use churchy words, but I do want to worship and praise You as You deserve. God, I know You're greater and larger than my mind could ever imagine. You're braver, smarter, stronger, and wiser than I could ever fathom. Thank You for Your gifts and blessings. Thanks for making me Your daughter—especially when I didn't deserve it. You've done more for me than I could imagine, because You are generous. You've forgiven more than I remember, because You're patient and merciful. You've taught me more than I have capacity to retain, because You're so wise. Thank You for taking the time with me even when I don't deserve it and don't show much potential. I want to praise You for being so great and more wonderful than our human minds could imagine. I want to praise You for Your creations here on earth. Just by looking at them, studying them, and understanding them, we get a greater glimpse of who You are and Your unsurpassable level of creativity. When I consider the human body, I realize that it's so intricate, only You could have created it. You had so much foresight. You created the Sabbath as a day of rest for us to set aside all the troubles of this world. Lord, I praise You now, even though I don't know how. Even though the concept is foreign to me, I praise You just because of who You are. Amen.

In many ways praise is actually for us. God already knows who He is. He already knows everything He's done. He's aware of His power and strength. But when we tell Him—saying it or writing it out—it lets us see ourselves in relation to God.

If there's one person in the Bible whose praise really spoke to the strength of his relationship with God, it's Job. While working on this chapter, I wondered to myself and prayed, asking God what the difference was with Job. Why was he so steady in his faith and how was he able to praise amid losing everything? Then one concept came to mind and challenged my perspective. It was the perception of being deserving.

During my year of studying Spanish in Spain, our professors made an amazing contrast between American students and Spanish students. When it comes to receiving grades, they observed that Americans have a "deserving" attitude—a sort of entitlement. Unlike schools in America, the Spanish grading scale rewards students with a number falling between 1 and 10, 10 being the highest score a student can receive and 1 being the lowest. It is uncommon for a large portion of the class to receive a 10 as a final grade. But because our program was in cooperation with American universities, we continued to be graded on the American grading scale of A through F. The majority of the American students, the professors observed, felt as though they deserved A's in every class, and to them this idea was incongruent with the purpose of a grading system. Whether it's true or not, this "deserving" attitude speaks volumes about our society. From birth we are bred for fairness—to get what we deserve, whether good or bad. As children we start out demanding fairness as we lobby our parents to give us the same favor as our siblings. This attitude then follows us to school, work, and church; we spread it everywhere we go until we have infected everyone around us with the idea that they too must receive what they deserve (or perceive they deserve).

Amazingly enough, God does *not* give us what we deserve. "You see, at just the right time, when we were still powerless, Christ died for the ungodly. Very rarely will anyone die for a righteous person, though for a good person someone might possibly dare to die. But God demonstrates his own love for us in this: While we were still sinners, Christ died for us" (Romans 5:6-8).

Just as God does not punish us as we deserve, He also does not bless us because we are "deserving." When Satan was still an angel of light in heaven, he had (and still has) a "deserving" attitude. Isaiah 14:12-14 explains it this way: "How you have fallen from heaven, morning star, son of the dawn! You have been cast down to the earth, you who once laid low the nations! You said in your heart, 'I will ascend to heaven; I will raise my throne above the stars of God; I will sit enthroned on the mount of assembly, on the utmost heights of the Mount Zaphon. I will ascend above the tops of the clouds; I will make myself like the Most High.'" Satan's strategy was to try to impose this deserving attitude on Job (and he tries to impose it on us as well).

As Job 1 describes, there was a meeting in heaven—and who shows up but Satan, the accuser. Upon his arrival, God addresses him, "'Where have you come from?' Satan answered the Lord, 'From roaming throughout the earth, going back and forth in it'" (verse 7). Then with the pride of a father pulling out his wallet to show off pictures of his kids, God asked Satan, "Have you considered my servant Job? There is no one on earth like him; he is blameless and upright, a man who fears God and shuns evil" (verse 8).

Let's pause right here. Every child loves it when their parents are proud of them. Parents enjoy their children being proud of them as well. For instance, for the past year my mom has been doing graduate coursework, and at the end of her last class she called eagerly to tell me she had earned an A (what did I tell you about American students and their grades?). And I was proud of her. Parents show their children (and children show their parents) their excitement and pride by proudly posting artwork, report cards, photos, etc., on their refrigerators. In a sense, that's what God did; he posted Job's record on display for everyone to see. This can be a point of pondering: Is your record such that God would take pride in displaying it?

But when God brought up Job, Satan immediately started taking jabs at him.

"Job doesn't obey you for nothing! You protect him. You made him rich. I guarantee if you took away all he had, he'd curse you to your face!"

Those were strong words—a challenge, even. But God was not alarmed. He was accustomed to Satan's temper tantrums. He knew His relationship with Job was solid, and unlike Satan, Job did not have a "deserving" attitude, so God responded, "Very well, then, everything he has is in your power, but on the man himself, do not lay a finger" (verse 12).

Satan probably rubbed his hands together gleefully and giggled. His evil mind began to conjure images of the disaster and destruction he could bring on Job. Best of all would be if he could get Job to blame it all on God. He loved when humans did that. So he went off immediately to carry out his plan. He had no interest in staying for the rest of the meeting to hear all of the good things God was doing in the universe, and to hear the praise and accolades He would receive.

Job was a very respected man in his community. Not only was he quite wealthy, but he had a large family and a certain calm about him. One day, however, a series of events that started as a spring shower spiraled out of control to become a category 5 hurricane.

Job's wealth was measured by all the livestock he owned. These animals were his currency. Not only did they provide clothing and food—they were also good for trading so he could get other things he needed.

The "spring shower" began when a messenger came to Job with some bad news: A large group of Sabeans came and took the oxen and donkeys at swordpoint. How a group of men stole 500 oxen and 500 donkeys I'm not sure, but the messenger was the only one to escape to tell about it. Job's heart began to beat a little faster. A small shot of adrenaline burst through his body.

Just as he was coming to terms with this news, the first messenger was interrupted by the staccato steps of another young man who abruptly landed in front of him. Job looked up in concern and urged the young man to speak. Fear was written on his face. He could hardly get the words to come out straight.

"The fire of God fell from the heavens and burned up the sheep and the servants, and I am the only one who has escaped to tell you" (verse 16).

Upon hearing that, Job's heart was in his mouth. His mind was attempting to wrap itself around all he was hearing. And while the messenger continued with the details of the story, another man ran up and interrupted the last.

"Job!" he yelled, out of breath. "The Chaldeans formed three raiding parties and stole all of your camels! I'm the only one who escaped to tell you."

With each delivery of bad news, Job felt as thought he was sinking deeper and deeper into the ground—but the last bit of news buried him.

"While he was still speaking, yet another messenger came and said, 'Your sons and daughters were feasting and drinking wine at the oldest brother's house, when suddenly a mighty wind swept in from the desert and struck the four corners of the house. It collapsed on them and they are dead, and I am the only one who has escaped to tell you!' At this, Job got up and tore his robe and shaved his head. Then he fell to the ground in worship and said: 'Naked I came from my mother's womb, and naked I will depart. The Lord gave and the Lord has taken away; may the name of the Lord be praised.' In all this, Job did not sin by charging God with wrongdoing" (verses 18-22).

Job did not have a "deserving" attitude. His praise was the result of knowing and understanding who God is. He understood that the things God did were supporting evidence of who He is, and for this reason, he was able to praise God no matter what. And there is much more to be learned through Job's experience than this summary here. I invite you to read the rest of the story to see how it ends.

When I was a kid, I often told God that I didn't have an experience with Him. I didn't understand who He was. Now I feel so loved. In fact, I feel swallowed up in love. What have I done to deserve such love? Absolutely nothing. That's the beauty of it. "While we were still sinners, Christ died for us" (Romans 5:8). That's the greatest reason of all to praise God—because *He* deserves it!

What are some practical ways you can praise Him?

- Through songs: Listen to music and sing songs that honor God.
- Battle stories: Share the way God has helped you fight a battle in your life.
- Read Scriptures of praise out loud. I've shared one of my recent favorites with you below:

Psalm 96

Sing to the Lord a new song;
sing to the Lord, all the earth.
Sing to the Lord, praise his name;
proclaim his salvation day after day.
Declare his glory among the nations,
his marvelous deeds among all peoples.
For great is the Lord and most worthy of praise;
he is to be feared above all gods.
For all the gods of the nations are idols,
but the Lord made the heavens.
Splendor and majesty are before him;
strength and glory are in his sanctuary.
Ascribe to the Lord, all you families of nations,
ascribe to the Lord glory and strength.
Ascribe to the Lord the glory due his name;
bring an offering and come into his courts.
Worship the Lord in the splendor of his holiness;
tremble before him, all the earth.
Say among the nations, "The Lord reigns."
The world is firmly established, it cannot be moved;
he will judge the peoples with equity.
Let the heavens rejoice, let the earth be glad;
let the sea resound, and all that is in it.
Let the fields be jubilant, and everything in them;
Let all the trees of the forest sing for joy.
Let all Creation rejoice before the Lord, for he comes,
he comes to judge the earth.
He will judge the world in righteousness
and the peoples in his faithfulness.

As I mentioned at the beginning of this chapter, the purpose of praise is the restoration of our relationship with God. When we praise God, we have a better idea of who He is, and it puts us in a better place for relationship building. God has given us many tools to build and restore our relationship with Him; however, a tool in the hand of someone who doesn't understand its purpose is useless. And this is what we'll discover in the next chapter. Understanding the purpose of praise is the perfect segue into understanding the Sabbath. Simply stated, the purpose of the Sabbath is relationship building and restoration—but unfortunately, not fully understanding this principle makes this powerful tool for relationship building as unappreciated as an Excel spreadsheet in the hands of a 5-year-old. The spreadsheet does not lose its value because of whose hands it's in, but the value of the spreadsheet is lost on the 5-year-old because they are unaware of its worth. And that's what we'll discover in the next chapter: How the value of the Sabbath can be lost on so many of us because we don't understand its worth.

The Young and the Rest-less

Learning to Enjoy Sabbath Rest: The Story of the Sabbath

Do you remember your first love—the way it sounded? the way it felt? Do you remember how much you used to laugh at everything the object of your affection said? Do you remember the long conversations, sometimes creeping up to an unbelievable hour? Do you remember when time was not enough, so much so that you wanted to steal memories from your past and put them in your present? Let me share with you with a refreshing truth: God longs to spend that kind of time with you. He longs to be in your presence and in your consciousness. He longs to get to know you intimately, and for you to know Him as well. When you open yourself to spending time with God, you are putting yourself in the perfect place for relationship building. ❧

When we read the Bible, it is evident that the overarching theme is telling us of a God of love who longs to be in a relationship with us. As we look at the subject of the Sabbath, we see that God set up the Sabbath as a way to encourage and promote that relationship. He has provided every way possible for us to bond with Him and spend time with Him. In His anticipation of building a relationship with us, God planned a date with us. To understand it in today's terms, let's say God set up a recurring event in His calendar for the seventh day of the week, every week of the year, for the rest of our lives. From the very beginning He had the foresight to set aside time to spend with us.

"By the seventh day God had finished the work he had been doing: so on the seventh day he rested from all his work. God blessed the seventh day and made it holy, because on it he rested from all the work of creating that he had done" (Genesis 2:2, 3).

The Sabbath was designed to protect our relationship with God. For this reason we see the Sabbath being established in the Garden of Eden and emphasized again with the children of Israel in the story of the manna. The Sabbath was then written in stone at Mount Sinai as part of the Ten Commandments, continuously observed through the time of Jesus and by His apostles even after His death.

I tried to explain the Sabbath to a friend of mine who grew up in a different religious persuasion from me. As we talked, I noticed that there was always something blocking his thinking in the conversation. He could hardly hear what I was saying because growing up, he had a friend whose family observed the Sabbath. At that time in his life the kids on his block always hung out together. They got their first bikes together and played together after school. On Friday afternoons, however, as the sun would begin to tuck itself away in the horizon, his friend's mother would always announce that it was time to come inside. The reason wasn't like the 1970s answer that children should be inside before dark; his friend was being called in because it was the Sabbath. Apparently this image always stuck in his mind, and his childhood self deemed the Sabbath as something that robbed kids of their fun.

Many years later, a few hours before the dawning of another Sabbath, this same friend called me, and the first thing that came out of his mouth was a question: Did I have the TV on? At the time I did, and I responded as such.

"Why?" he asked. "Isn't it the Sabbath?"

I told him the Sabbath had not quite arrived (and although it had not, I realize I should have been preparing for its arrival). I suppose I answered him on a technicality. From there he asked about the Sabbath and my other beliefs. Although previously I had longed to share with him what I believed, in that moment I was gripped by fear—especially the fear of rejection. Isn't that a common reaction many of us experience? Aren't we all, at one time or another, gripped by fear? The next time you find yourself in this situation, remember, this fear is not of God, "for the Spirit God gave us does not make us timid, but gives us power, love and self-discipline" (2 Timothy 1:7).

Thinking back, if I were to have the opportunity to speak with my friend again, I would have the courage to say that God is a God of love and that He created the Sabbath out of love. Our observation and celebration of the day is our expression of love back to Him, the same way we express our love to a boyfriend or a girlfriend through dates and gifts. Think about it—whenever you begin a new relationship, you learn the other person's preferences. As a man, you might ask a woman her favorite flowers, and as a woman, you may ask a man his favorite food. The popular author Gary Chapman calls these our love languages. Jesus let us know His love language in John 14:15, "If you love me, keep my commands." He doesn't say this so that we can make it to heaven; he asks for it as an expression of our love to Him.

If I were to have the opportunity to speak with my friend again, I would explain to him that in keeping the sanctity of the day I am also preserving the sanctity of my relationship with God. What do I mean by this? Everybody knows that Friday nights and Saturdays are big days to go out, play sports, or engage in other social activities. It's not that those of us who observe the Sabbath are not aware of this, nor do we think these activities are not fun or good. On the contrary, I used be sad when I'd miss the end of *Family Matters* when I was a kid. For all I know, Steve Urkel might have convinced Laura to love him after I turned off the TV. But God asked me to keep the Sabbath day holy. Is *Family Matters* more important to me than what He asked me to do? The point of the Sabbath is to engage in activities that promote our relationships with God. As we celebrate, we learn to prioritize our relationship with God over other relationships.

Too many people either live or have witnessed a Christianity devoid of Christ. The same is true of the Sabbath. The Sabbath without a relationship with God is useless. It turns a holy day into an obligation. It's a gift, but many of us don't know what to do with it. The saddest part is that within the Christian community, the Sabbath discussion has become more about theology than about love. We're like a group of kids bickering over their parents' estate after their death. Instead of enjoying what's been bestowed to us, we're fighting over it. God longs to give us perfection, but we're settling for what we think is "good enough." In giving us the Sabbath, God longed to give us a gift—a time to rest and enjoy his presence. He even said so, in Mark 2:27, "The Sabbath was made for man, not man for the Sabbath."

Perhaps you're thinking it's "good enough" for me to spend some time with God whenever I can whether Monday or Tuesday or Thursday. I'll have a quick morning prayer, ask Him for protection and His blessing over the day; however, God longs to give you perfection. In a world full of gadgets, gizmos and whatchamacallits, God simply wants us to rest. And the gift of rest He has given us in the Bible can be found in His weekly Sabbath on the seventh day of the week.

I understand we come from different places, different denominations, and different levels of faith and maturity in our relationship with God. Some of us have no faith at all, but somehow we ultimately want the same thing. We want God to show up, and be real and apparent. And the more we seek God and ask Him what he wants from us, the clearer He will become to us.

While I was in college, my uncle helped me prepare for life in the working world by teaching me to be a gopher with initiative. You know what a gopher is, right? Or maybe I should say a gofer. A gofer is a person who's in the early stages of her career whose responsibility it is to "go for" things. Get the papers off of the copy machine or go for the team's lunch. My uncle taught me to understand the "whys" of what I was doing and to anticipate my boss's needs. He emphasized to me that I shouldn't just work, I should try to understand why I do the things I do.

Have you done the same? Do you think about why you do the things you do? Perhaps you've grown up observing the Sabbath or maybe this is the first time you're hearing about it. Perhaps you go to church on another day. In any case it's important to understand why we do the things we do, and even more important, through this we'll learn what God wants us to do. Let's explore the history of God's Sabbath and see why it's important to Him that we observe and celebrate it with Him each week.

As I mentioned in chapter 4, my dad grew up sharecropping in Alabama. I knew this because he used to tell me stories about his childhood. During family vacations to Huntsville I used to listen intensely as my aunts and uncles shared funny stories about each other, school, and their experiences on the farm. While initially I was embarrassed about my last name, Lemons, because there were so many jokes one could make with it, over time, as I began to understand the history behind it, I began to wear the name with pride. I knew where I came from. When we had school projects that required us to put together a family tree, I gladly filled in the blanks with the names of as many of my ancestors as I could find. I loved to hear a relative tell me that I was a good storyteller like my grandmother or to hear far-fetched tales about various relatives from my uncle. Similar to what we learned in chapter 5 about praise, we are better able to understand *who* we are when we understand *where* we come from. The same is true of our Christian faith; it's important that we understand where we come from. When you understand this, you'll have a better understanding of who you are.

Can you imagine the dawning of the first Sabbath? It must be recorded as the *best* first date in history. Adam and Eve and God explored the beautiful planet God had just made. Eve, in all of her curiosity, wanted to know about everything—every butterfly that flitted by, the smell of every exquisite flower, the taste of all of the fruit, the mischievous glint in the eye of the chipmunks, and the delightful squeals of the sea creatures as they explored their new homes. Most of all, can you imagine the Adam and Eve's excitement as they got to know their Creator for the first time? They basked in His love and His attention. They marveled at His kindness. They were so attracted to Him; it was almost as though He were magnetic. They never wanted to leave His presence.

Though circumstances changed, the Sabbath, and its power to bring humans close to God, continued throughout time, all the way until we arrive at our next stop in history.

Let's do a little digging by looking at one of the most familiar periods in Christian history: the Reformation. We'll begin with Martin Luther, a German monk with the Augustinian order in the early sixteenth century. Many people recognize him as the one who posted his 95 theses on the door of the church of Wittenberg. And while this may appear to be church-style guerrilla warfare, with Luther attempting to stir up controversy, it was actually his way of starting a discussion. He wanted to get the powers that be to address the issues he saw had the potential to eat away at the core of the Catholic Church. Luther was sincere in his efforts. In fact, long before he addressed the external conflict he was witnessing, he battled with an internal conflict.

During this internal conflict, he began examining his relationship with God, and he saw it as anything but loving. He had grown to view God as angry and always ready to punish him, and his environment may have significantly influenced this thinking. Within the Catholic Church it was commonly taught that the day after you confessed your sins, a penance should be done in an effort to right your wrong. To take the concept of penances a step further, indulgences were being sold as a replacement to penances. Indulgences were pieces of paper the sinner could purchase to take away their sins, or supposedly decrease the amount of time a loved one would have to spend in purgatory (according to Catholic teaching, the middle ground that sits between heaven and hell).

To Luther, this logic made God seem like a Payday Loan store, keeping tabs on sinners' debts that continuously grew because of outrageous interest. These practices, along with the perspective he gained from his studies, shaped Luther's thinking of God as more similar to a shrewd moneylender than a loving Savior, and this put Luther in a place of fear. And who wouldn't be scared of a God like that? Luther was bothered by the idea of God; the very thought of God made him nervous.

Luther had to know if the way he perceived God was true, so he began to search the Bible. In doing so, he discovered a very different picture of God. He found a God that didn't charge interest on humanity's debt from sin. In fact, He found a God who paid the price Himself. Luther could no longer match up the practices of indulgences and penances with his new understanding of God, so in keeping with his desire to do right and help the church, he told Albert of Mainz, the archbishop in his area, of all that was taking place—especially the practice of selling indulgences. Luther was convinced that once Mainz knew what was happening in his territory he would immediately try to straighten things out.

Mainz did react immediately, but not as Luther expected. He immediately forwarded Luther's new understanding to the headquarters in Rome—not in an effort to help Luther find resolution, but because Luther's actions stepped on Mainz's toes. In a roundabout way, Mainz was not only aware of the issue of indulgences, but also benefitting from them (as were many others, including the church itself). Some of the funds earned through indulgences were being used to help pay for the building of a cathedral called St. Peter's Basilica.

At the same time that Luther sent his newfound view to the archbishop, he also sent it to the printer. In those days there were no strict copyright restrictions, so when printers realized material was popular, they printed and sold it. I'm sure that when Luther sent his work to the printer, he didn't anticipate the response he would receive. The information spread at an alarmingly fast pace; within weeks numerous printers got hold of the document and distributed it, until Luther's theses were floating around Spain, Italy, the Netherlands, and France.

Remember that throughout all this, Luther wasn't hoping to start his own church or movement. He simply wanted resolution *within* the Catholic Church. However, upon receipt and review of Luther's document, tongues began to wag and heads began to shake. The church sensed the impact Luther's challenge could have on the church body, and they invited him to attend the Diet of Worms to recant or take back his statements. Contrary to how the name sounds, the Diet of Worms was a meeting held in Worms, a small town located in present-day Germany. During this meeting Luther not only failed to recant, but spoke the following bold and inspiring words:

"Unless I am convinced by the testimonies of the Holy Scriptures or evident reason (for I believe in neither the Pope nor councils alone, since it has been established that they have often erred and contradicted themselves), I am bound by the Scriptures that I have adduced, and my conscience has been taken captive by the Word of God; and I am neither able nor willing to recant, since it is neither safe nor right to act against conscience. God help me. Amen."[1]

After this meeting, all doubts about Luther's position were cleared. With his spoken words he had reinforced his written words and as a result he was declared a heretic, or a believer who holds contrary beliefs to those of his church.

By this point the church had declared its stance on Luther, and though it was obvious how they felt about his theses, they still had not officially addressed his claims. In fact, many years went by before the church formally met to address this uprising that was occurring in their midst as a result of Luther's discovery.

The lack of response was not because the church didn't try to address the issue. Between the years of 1545 to 1563 the Council of Trent, the meeting designed to address Luther's claim and develop a formal opinion, convened and adjourned several times for a variety of reasons. However, no conclusion was made.

Why was this meeting important? To put the whole situation in perspective, imagine that someone makes an accusation against you. As a result you will respond either to agree or disagree with what was said. The same was true in this case; Luther posed his accusations against the church in his 95 theses. And while the Catholic Church responded by declaring him a heretic, it didn't officially address his claims until it issued a declaration from the Council of Trent.

By the time the final session of the Council of Trent convened in 1563, Luther had passed away 17 years prior. Instead of working toward reconciliation, as Luther had hoped, the council made a declaration on the Catholic Church's position and its beliefs that directly opposed Luther's findings. While Luther's call was for a church that was based on *sola scriptura*, or the Bible alone, at the Council of Trent, the Catholic Church reinforced its belief of a church based on the Bible *and* tradition. We'll explore this idea a little bit later.

Do you think it matters to God when we worship Him? Whether it's Friday, Saturday, or Sunday, we're still getting in some quality time with Him, right?

When Jesus was on earth, He boldly did the things He believed God wanted Him to do, and this ruffled a lot of feathers. During His time the powers that be, the Pharisees and the Sadducees, hated Him. He was rocking the boat and calling them out on all of the shady practices they had been carrying out.

One day a group of Pharisees, or the religious leaders of that time, came up to Jesus hoping to stump Him or at least to get Him to say the wrong thing. "'Teacher,' they said, 'we know that you are a man of integrity and that you teach the way of God in accordance with the truth. You aren't swayed by others, because you pay no attention to who they are. Tell us then, what is your opinion? Is it right to pay the imperial tax to Caesar or not?' But Jesus, knowing their evil intent, said, 'You hypocrites, why are you trying to trap me? Show me the coin used for paying the tax.' They brought him a denarius, and he asked them, 'Whose image is this? And whose insciption?' 'Caesar's,' they replied. Then he said to them, 'So give back to Caesar what is Caesar's, and to God what is God's'" (Matthew 22:16-21). In our love relationship with God, we should speak His love language, and give back to Him what He asks from us. We should love Him in the way He asks to be loved.

Imagine you are married. What type of reaction would you expect from your wife if she asked to go out for Chinese and you took her out for Italian instead? Or if your anniversary were on January 25, would it be OK with her if you went out together on January 30 instead? Would it be OK to give the excuse that at least you celebrated a day with her? Should she just be happy that the two of you spent time together? It's the same in our relationship with God: He asks us to show our love toward Him in a very specific way. God created the seventh-day Sabbath as His day of worship, and He wants us to worship Him during this time "in the Spirit and in truth" (John 4:24).

One time I attended the church service of a large well-known non-denominational congregation in Texas. The sanctuary was mammoth in size and filled to the brim with people. The music was engaging, and the speaker was inspirational. As I glanced around at the congregants, I saw many with the same look of sincerity etched on their faces as I had witnessed in Brazil while studying abroad. I'm sure God loved and appreciated their worship. Even still, God wants us to worship Him as He has asked, *when* He has asked. Just as He spoke to the Pharisees that day when they questioned Him about Caesar's taxes, He speaks to us: Please, give Me what I ask for. Are we truly giving God what He has asked for?

At the Council of Trent the Catholic Church gave its opinions on many things (at the time of publication, a copy of the catechism from this council could be found on the University of Toronto's library Web site). We already know that it didn't come down on the side with Luther. At this meeting the church also gave its opinion about something else—the Sabbath. On page 267 of the summary written from the council it says, "But the Church of God has in her wisdom ordained that the celebration of the Sabbath should be transferred to 'the Lord's day': as on that day light first shone on the world, so by the resurrection of our Lord on the same day, by whom was thrown open to us the gate to eternal life, we were called out of darkness into light; and hence the Apostle would have it called 'the Lord's day.'"[2]

Luther and others did well to stand up for the cause of following the Scriptures and the Scriptures alone. As a result he, and others, started movements separate from the Catholic Church, and while they broke away from many of the practices of the Catholic Church, the idea of worshipping on Sunday, which was authorized at the Council of Trent, instead of Saturday managed to sneak its way into their teaching.

As we discussed, God longs to give us perfection, but often we think we're satisfied with "good enough." What does this mean? It means that God wants to give us something of tremendous value. It means that God longs to give us something authentic.

While on a trip to visit a friend in South Korea, I decided to visit Dongdaemun, a local open-air market. My senses were assaulted from every angle; this was no Disneyworld visit with slick tourist attractions. This was the real deal. Each section of the market was organized by the type of merchandise it sold. There was a section for kitchenware, for clothing, for souvenirs, and, after I wandered down a labyrinth of alleys, a section for purses. As I passed by each booth in the purse section the vendors yelled out in attempts to entice me to enter their stores. Finally I paused at one of the booths to inspect a wallet. As I glanced at the saleswoman I saw a flash of light cross her eyes, as though she had just come upon a wonderful idea.

"I show you good one!" she said enticingly with her choppy, heavily accented English.

I shrugged nonchalantly, not knowing what "good one" meant but remaining open to soaking in the experience. To my surprise, she pulled out a long silver rod with a hook on the end and began fishing in the ceiling racks. I looked up to see what she might catch. I was surprised to see a school of purses swimming in the ceiling. The one she caught and proudly showed me was a Louis Vuitton handbag. Actually, let's say it was *inspired* by Louis. I glanced at it and declined to buy it, only to have her offer me several similar items before I politely exited her shop.

In contrast, during Christmas break from my school in Spain, I remember backpacking through Paris. I was so starstruck by the experience. I didn't have to do much—I was simply happy to be there (though I was a broke college student who lived off of bread, cheese, and juice and didn't have money to do much else besides just be there). As my friend and I walked the Champs-Élysées we took notice of the Louis Vuitton store as it proudly stood guard on the corner like a sentinel, brightly decorated. While the store in South Korea that was hidden away in the cut of the alley, this store was clearly marked and boldly sported the official Louis Vuitton signage. The facade of the building was befitting that of a luxury brand.

As we continued our walk (one of the few free things we could do) a couple approached us, though the woman did most of the talking. She spoke in an English that was speckled with remnant sounds from her native tongue. Dragging our oversized bags all around town, we were clearly (poor) college student tourists. The woman had the most suspicious proposition, and as she presented it to us, she held a wad of Euros in her hand. I took turns looking at her and then at the money. Guess what she asked: If we would go inside the Louis Vuitton store and purchase two handbags for her, she would compensate us for our efforts. Though we were broke, we weren't desperate; and in the end we declined her offer.

It wasn't until later that I better understood the reason behind her request. For years the Louis Vuitton brand had worked to establish a market in Asia. The purchase per household was limited at the Champ-Élysées store in Paris for fear that people would buy multiple bags and resell them in Asia, causing their value to decline. For this reason Louis Vuitton has made every effort to zealously guard the value of its brand, knowing that it must battle bootleggers, counterfeiters, and those that were out to decrease the value of the brand.

The same is true with God's Sabbath. Sometimes we attempt to devalue God's day. Perhaps we know about the Sabbath, but we don't observe and celebrate it as we should. Or maybe we're satisfied with "good enough," and we want to continue worshipping on another day because this is what we've always done. Whatever the case, He does everything He can to zealously guard His brand and to protect our relationship with Him.

The seventh-day Sabbath is God's real deal. Like anything authentic, it boldly bears God's brand. A quick review of it in Exodus 20:8 teaches us that the first word God uses when referring to the Sabbath is the word "remember," but so often we forget it. In the commandment God places His stamp of ownership on the day, stating that "the seventh day is a sabbath to the Lord your God." Then He qualifies the day, or tells us how He feels about the day.

In the last line of the commandment He says, "Therefore the Lord blessed the Sabbath day and made it holy." Just as the Louis Vuitton brand is easily recognizable, after we read this commandment it is just as easy to identify God's brand on this day as well. The Sabbath zealously stands like a sentinel in an effort to protect our relationship with God by setting aside a day as a reminder for us to rest. Whether we acknowledge it or not, we are a rest-less society, and through the Sabbath the Lord offers us rest. Not just physical rest, but spiritual rest as well.

"Take my yoke upon you and learn from me, for I am gentle and humble in heart, and you will find rest for your souls" (Matthew 11:29).

The issue is one of authenticity. The difference is as distinct as buying the authentic Louis Vuitton bag on the Champs-Élysées in Paris versus buying the imitation in a cubbyhole store in an unidentified shop in South Korea.

I've heard it said in conversations with friends, in books, on the Internet, and on TV that this concept of keeping the Sabbath is not for Christians of this day and age. After reading this, some of you may agree that spending time with God is a crucial part of your relationship with them, but you still believe that the Sabbath is vintage—that it's for another time and another group of people. Whatever your belief system, I'd like to explore this idea. As you read I'd like to suggest that the Sabbath was made especially for you.

Have you heard of the old and new covenants in the Bible? A covenant is basically a two-sided promise—you keep your end of the deal, and I'll keep mine. They stretch throughout the Old and New Testaments. They are at the heart of understanding the Bible; understanding them helps to put us in the perfect place for relationship building.

The covenants help us see two perspectives of how we can approach our relationship with God. Within the old covenant we take our spiritual lives in our own hands. Like a small child, just getting a little bit of hand-eye coordination, we push our parents' hands away as they try to help us tie our shoes or steady our hand while we attempt to feed ourselves. On the other hand, under the new covenant, we acknowledge our need for God and admit that in this crazy world, we are unable to make it on our own—we need God's help and guidance. We see these two scenarios played out in the lives of two Bible stories—the children of Israel and Abraham.

The Old Covenant

Three months after the children of Israel escaped slavery in Egypt, they arrived in the Desert of Sinai and camped in front of a mountain by the same name—Mount Sinai. Moses went up to the top of the mountain to talk with God, and God told him to make sure the people were spiritually ready, because He was about to do something very special. Then, just as He promised, God met Moses at the top of the mountain and gave him the Ten Commandments to give to the children of Israel.

Did sin exist before Moses received the Ten Commandments? Of course! We know Cain killed Abel, there was great wickedness during the time of Noah, God destroyed Sodom and Gomorrah for its sinfulness, etc. And "where there is no law there is no transgression" (Romans 4:15). So we know that the law existed before this time. However, because the children of Israel had been in slavery for 430 years, God needed to give them some living guidelines. He needed to make them conscious of sin (as explained in Romans 3:20). After the Ten Commandments were given, a covenant or a two-way promise was established.

"When Moses went and told the people all the Lord's words and laws, they responded with one voice, 'Everything the Lord has said we will do.' Moses then wrote down everything the Lord had said" (Exodus 24:3, 4). "Moses took half of the blood and put it in bowls, and the other half he splashed against the altar. Then he took the Book of the Covenant and read it to the people. They responded, 'We will do everything the Lord has said; we will obey.' Moses then took the blood, sprinkled it on the people and said, 'This is the blood of the covenant that the Lord has made with you in accordance with all these words'" (verses 6-8). After the people made the promise, Moses sealed the promise with the blood of bulls.

In that moment the children of Israel had taken on a heavier load than they could carry. Just like toddlers who are just learning their way around the world and need their parents' help, the children of Israel needed God's help to keep the law—none of us can keep it without God's help. Abraham, on the other hand, was very aware of this when he faced a similar situation.

The New Covenant

The new covenant was established with Abraham well before the old covenant. The idea behind the new covenant is that God made a promise and it is His responsibility to keep it. The burden is on Him (1 Peter 5:7). God's promise was much better than the promise the children of Israel made because it was a promise of a Savior. In fact, God "announced the gospel in advance to Abraham: 'All nations will be blessed through you'" (Galatians 3:8). Paul further emphasized this idea in verse 16: "The promises were spoken to Abraham and to his seed. Scripture does not say 'and to seeds,' meaning many people, but 'and to your seed,' meaning one person, who is Christ." We see this idea expressed in verses 17, 18: "The law, introduced 430 years later, does not set aside the covenant previously established by God and thus do away with the promise. For if the inheritance depends on the law, then it no longer depends on the promise; but God in his grace gave it to Abraham through a promise."

The new covenant holds a promise of rest, just like the Sabbath. Instead of trying to obey the law in our own strength, as the old covenant requires, we are now freed of our burden through the promise of the new covenant because Christ is responsible.

In these two scenarios we see two different ways we can approach our relationship with God, either as dependent on Him to help us live in the way He wants us to live, or independent as we struggle with certain failure because we are unable to keep the rules all by ourselves. Some see this newfound freedom we find in the new covenant as freeing us from the obligations of the Sabbath, but to look at the Sabbath in this way is to miss the point of why God established the Sabbath. The freedom the new covenant *does* offer us is the freedom of the obligations of the old covenant.

"When you were dead in your sins and in the uncircumcision of your flesh, God made you alive with Christ. He forgave us all our sins, having canceled the charge of our legal indebtedness, which stood against us and condemned us; he has taken it away, nailing it to the cross" (Colossians 2:13, 14).

"The law is only a shadow of the good things that are coming—not the realities themselves. For this reason it can never, by the same sacrifices repeated endlessly year after year, make perfect those who draw near to worship" (Hebrews 10:1).

Contrary to popular thought, Christ's death did not nail the Sabbath to the cross. In fact, Christ's death was further support for the Sabbath. The new covenant was sealed at His death. Through this act He gave us another break from the burdens of life. Both the Sabbath and the new covenant emphasize the idea that we can rest in God for our salvation. Jesus taught us time and time again throughout His life that the true purpose of the Sabbath is to restore our relationship with Him.

Jesus entered the synagogue, as He did each Sabbath. His eyes quickly scanned the room; He saw many faces He recognized, though not all for good reasons. He knew many people were out to get Him, but even still He carried Himself with purpose.

Almost magnetically His attention was drawn to one man seated in the middle of the room. Jesus spotted an empty space behind him and quickly settled in. Though as He entered He hardly disturbed the dust on the floor, all eyes landed on Him as He took His seat. A low murmur stirred in the room. Many noticed that He had taken a seat behind the man with the withered hand. Jesus had a reputation—one that the sick spoke about hopefully and that the religious leaders murmured about jealously. Surely this Jesus character would not be so bold as to heal the man *in* the synagogue *on* the Sabbath, or would He? Without so much as flinching, as eyes curiously flickered back and forth, first on Him and then on the man, Jesus spoke to the man with the withered hand. His voice was altogether kind yet carried the weight of authority. "Stand up," He told the man. While many had come to the synagogue out of routine that morning, a sermon was being played out right before their very eyes. "Which is lawful on the Sabbath: to do good or to do evil, to save a life or to kill?" Though only seconds before, the religious leaders were overflowing with words and insults, at this moment their mouths were filled with silence. Jesus peered at each one individually. His look was piercing—it shot through their eyes and looked into their hearts, and he perceived coldness. He perceived hearts that were hardened to the love of God. With a calm power Jesus commanded the man, "'Stretch out your hand.' He stretched it out, and his hand was completely restored" (Mark 3:1-5).

Just as Jesus restored the man's hand, the Sabbath was created to restore our relationship with Him. It was also created so we may restore our relationships with one another. Just as the old and new covenants help us put our relationship with God in perspective, so too does the Sabbath. God longs for us to see the Sabbath as the very foundation of our relationship with Him.

Get Some Rest

There's a common phrase my mom would always say to me as a child: "Rai, go lie down. You look tired. You need some rest." Sometimes I couldn't discern if she genuinely wanted me to get some sleep or if *she* needed some rest from *me*. Either way the idea is there: We all need rest. God foresaw this and created the Sabbath for all of humanity from the beginning of time. Now the question is *How* should we spend this time with Him? I've provided a few ideas below:

Spend Time With Other Believers

"Let us . . . not give up meeting together, as some are in the habit of doing, but encouraging one another—and all the more as you see the Day approaching" (Hebrews 10:24, 25).

It's encouraging to belong to a church family and to know that people are concerned about you. One of the things I appreciate about my childhood is that I belonged to a community of people who were genuinely concerned with my growth and wellbeing. They were familiar with my goals and experiences and beyond encouraging along the way. More than once they gave me a standing ovation for something I did at the church, whether playing the piano, singing, or acting. And I'll be the first to tell you that I don't belong on Broadway. There's something special about joining a group of people to worship God on the Sabbath.

Do Something Special for God

The Sabbath is a good time to reach out to your neighbors. It doesn't have to be the only time you do it, but it's a day you will most likely have more time than other days to express your love to God and to others. The best way to reach out is to assess the needs in your community. Is there a large group of young people? Start building relationships with them on Sabbath and develop a basketball or tutoring program for them during the week. Are there senior communities? Go by their rooms and read to them, interact with them, and let them know they are not forgotten.

Spend Time Strengthening Relationships With Others

Spend time with your families and friends. Mend broken relationships. As we discussed prayer in chapter 4, we sometimes hinder the development of our relationship with God because of how we treat our relationships with others.

Rest

Take some time to rest both physically and spiritually. Enjoy the day. Visit nature. This may vary depending on where you live. Enjoy the ocean, mountains, forests, or the snow. Whatever piece of nature you are afforded, learn to see God in it. Too many people who claim to observe the Sabbath find themselves running every which way on that day. God has given us rest, so take time to enjoy who God is and do what He has asked you to do: rest.

This may all be new and foreign information to you, or you may have heard it all before. Either way, I challenge you to view the Bible in light of God's love. Understand that through the Bible we see that God acted out of love, and His creation of the Sabbath day was no different. View the Sabbath as a gift. Accepting His gift puts you in the perfect place for relationship building. Doing so will help you learn to keep the fire alive in your relationship with God.

---

[1] *Luther's Works,* vol. 32, p. 112.

[2] J. Donovan, "The Catechism of the Council of Trent," *Canadian Libraries,* Aug. 27, 2009, p. 267; www.archive.org/details/thecatechismofth00donouoft.

Keeping the Fire Alive

Maintaining a Relationship With God: The Story of Hosea

After a long bout of no communication with a friend of mine from college, we sparked up a friendship and a routine of regular conversations after work. He'd gush about his day, the problems he'd encountered and short quips about people that quickly sparked my interest. His style was easy and carefree, though immediately serious when necessary.

I enjoyed the first conversation we had, though I didn't expect there would be others. I figured we were two friends catching up on life after a lull of communication. But he called me the next day, and the next, until slowly we developed a routine. Soon our conversations began to be one of the highlights of my day. This carried on for a week, and soon it spilled over into the next as well. I was beginning to get used to this. In fact, within my mind I had already planned a trip to visit this guy, who I thought had beau potential. It would be fun; it would bring to life all of the places and people he had so intricately described during our phone conversations.

One weekend, while visiting my BFF, I began to casually speak of my renewed friendship with Mr. Mention. In doing so, I logged on to a familiar networking site to back up my claim by showing her a picture of him. But the moment I clicked on his name and opened his page I felt as if I had been hit with a pile of bricks. I quickly pressed the back button on my browser. Surely there was a mistake. Though this looked like *my* Mr. Mention, this guy had the fateful words "in a relationship" next to his name. Couldn't be. Not after the conversations we had shared. He and I clicked; it couldn't be true. I tried again. Perhaps this famed networking site was experiencing an error of some sort. But a second attempt revealed, to my horror, that my potential interest was already attached to another. My heart sank. I scanned his page in curiosity and shock. Eventually I closed it, disallowing healthy curiosity to morph into unhealthy anger.

I sulked around for a few days as I prepared what I would say to Mr. Mention. But as time passed without the opportunity for our fateful conversation, I pondered the thought that perhaps I'm not that much different from my disappointer.

How many times had I delayed in introducing God to my friends and family? How often had I put off letting others know that I too am "in a relationship"? How often have the words I said misrepresented who God is? How often have I laughed at jokes at which Jesus would have shaken His head? How many opportunities have I passed by to help those around me, to feed the hungry and reach out to the lonely? Every time I do this, I am denying my relationship with God.

Not long after, I learned that relationships are God's gift to us. Not simply because they provide us with human companionship, but because they give us an opportunity to conceptualize our relationship with God. From the beginning of time we see that one of the first emotions Adam, the first man, experienced was loneliness. As Adam took on the monumental task of naming all the animals (Genesis 2:19, 20) he noticed that every creature had a mate. In that moment he discovered what it felt like *not* to have someone in his life. "So the man gave names to all the livestock, the birds of the sky and all the wild animals of the field. But for Adam no suitable helper was found" (verse 20).

While it's easy to gloss over this detail of the story, it actually reveals a lot about human nature and the character of God. We can all relate to the feeling of loneliness. Whether you are a stay-at-home mom surrounded by children but longing for a connection with your husband or peers, a middle-age recent divorcé, or a recent graduate in a foreign country, surrounded by the press of the crowd but longing to hear someone say something familiar, we can all identify with the feeling of loneliness. It is a greedy emotion because it not only depresses you, but also leaves you with a void.

While everything looks grim in this emotion, God can actually use it to help us conceptualize our lives without Him. Sometimes we know how to identify loneliness in our spiritual lives only through experiences we have in our human relationships. Loneliness is like the little gas indicator light in your car. It's an alert that lets you know it's time to refill the fuel of your relationship. When we see the indicator light in our vehicles come on, it's undeniable that we need to refill our tanks with gasoline. Neither water, soda, nor wiper fluid will do—only gasoline will suffice to keep the engine running. Why is it then that when we are left to identify the cause of loneliness in our spiritual lives, we attribute it to everything but God? We attempt to fill our lives with things that are just as insufficient at keeping our lives running, though they may offer a quick fix. But God longs for us to identify that emptiness in our hearts as a desire for Him.

While loneliness is a strong indicator that can be used, it is not the only human feeling with which God can speak to our hearts. Look at any of the human relationships you have in your life. Think of all the issues you deal with in those relationships. Equate the feelings you have within them with the feelings you have in your relationship with God. Although this is a flawed picture of our relationship with God, it does give us a glimpse into some of the common failings we have and some of the frustrations God must feel.

So are you like my Mr. Mention? Have you been faithful in *your* relationship with God? Have you been open with those around you by letting them know you are "in a relationship"?

After we come to understand the power of human relationships, it's a bit clearer why God decided to use the relationship of Gomer and Hosea to help the children of Israel (and us as well) conceptualize our relationship with Him. Maybe Gomer hadn't initially intended to be unfaithful to Hosea, but a few unguarded glances paired with enticing flirtations led many to believe she was unattached. However, over time she became brazen in her infidelity, saying, "I will go after my lovers" (Hosea 2:5).

Not to say the blame was all on Gomer, either. Out of all the girls Hosea could have chosen, he picked the one with all the red flags (Hosea 1:2). Prior to marriage she gave every indication that she would not be faithful. Yet in making this seemingly foolish choice, Hosea obeyed God's command.

Have you ever asked a couple the story of how they met? It's funniest when each person tells the story from their perspective, making sure to show themselves in the best light possible. I wonder how Hosea and Gomer would tell the story of how they became a couple. Would they hide the fact that Gomer was promiscuous, or would they abstain from sharing the details of her past (and present) life? God took all this into consideration, however. Before their marriage, "when the Lord began to speak by Hosea, the Lord said to Hosea: 'Go, take yourself a wife of harlotry and children of harlotry, for the land has committed great harlotry by departing from the Lord'" (verse 2, NKJV). Together they had three children, though rumor has it that Hosea wasn't involved in the "production" of all three.

If you haven't noticed by now, Hosea was having trouble at home, and it had everything to do with his trouble at work. As God's prophet, he was given the job of going out and representing God to Israel—and this wasn't a cushy desk job. Hosea 1 reveals that by the time God chose Hosea to speak, Israel was already in a bad way.

"This is the message that came to Hosea, the son of Beeri, during the reign of the kings of Judah from Uzziah to Hezekiah and during the reign of Jeroboam II, king of Israel" (Hosea 1:1, Clear Word). This verse doesn't tell us much until we do a bit of digging. In my own study I had to draw a time line to wrap my mind around it all. And in order to get an accurate picture of the sticky situation Hosea was stepping into, I had to dig through the books of 1-2 Kings and 1-2 Chronicles, most specifically in 2 Chronicles 26-29 and 2 Kings 14.

Israel and Judah had an on-again, off-again relationship with God, and it often started with their leadership. Uzziah (also known as Azariah in 2 Kings 15) started off his kingship well at the age of 16. He was actually faithful to God for a long time, and Judah did well under his reign during that time. However, as time went on he stopped playing the role he was given.

In chapter 5, which dealt with praise, we talked about roles in relationships. God also set up roles among the children of Israel. He chose the sons of Aaron from the tribe of Levi to act as priests, carrying out the priestly work in the sanctuary. Somewhere in the middle of his journey with God, Uzziah started getting a bit too comfortable and began to think he could do whatever he wanted without consequences. One day he entered the Temple and began burning incense, an act that symbolized the people's prayers going up to heaven. Although he was the king, it was not his role to perform duties in the sanctuary—it was strictly for the priesthood. So a large group of priests, 81 to be exact, confronted him and told him that he was in the wrong. This didn't sit well with Uzziah. Even though he knew what he did was wrong, he still had the audacity to get angry with the priests, and as he did, leprosy appeared all over his body (2 Kings 15:1-7 and 2 Chronicles 26).

Because of Uzziah's disobedience, his son Jotham took over the throne at age 25. Much as his father had done at the beginning of his kingship, Jotham did what was right and honored God. He ruled successfully for 16 years. Ahaz, on the other hand, who ruled after Jotham, seemed to undo the hard work that Uzziah and Jotham had accomplished. He managed to lose Judah's territory to the king of Assyria, and worse still, he led Judah to worship false gods. In God's eyes this was the worst way His people could cheat on Him and be unfaithful in their relationship. Under King Hezekiah, who followed King Ahaz, Judah saw spiritual reform, as Hezekiah made efforts to reopen the Temple. He was intensely focused on making Judah sovereign again.

Simultaneously, while this was going on in Judah, Israel was being led by Jeroboam II (2 Kings 14:23-29). He was in the twenty-seventh year of his reign when Uzziah began ruling in Judah. The Bible records that Jeroboam II was an evil king, in the same way the first King Jeroboam had been.

This is the background upon which the story of Hosea is painted. In an effort to explain to His people the way He viewed their cheating ways, God allowed this dramatic situation with Hosea to take place.

In looking at Gomer (and in looking at myself), I imagine that sometimes she had every intention of letting others know that she had a man at home, but somehow the words never seemed to pass her lips before she found herself in another sticky situation. In chapter 3 we learned about falling in love with Jesus. We learned that the initial phase of falling in love is the process of having our curiosity piqued about someone. There's something as sweet as cotton candy about the feeling that new love brings. Perhaps it's in knowing you're the apple of someone's eye, or maybe it's the sweetness of knowing that someone would do anything for you. "Greater love has no one than this: to lay down one's life for one's friends" (John 15:13).

But why does the love wane in our relationships with God? Why is it hard to maintain the high of an emotionally charged experience you had with God in the past? Why do the fascination and sense of enthrallment eventually wear off? I would suggest that it's hard to keep the love alive in a relationship in which you're not actively involved. In the Bible Jesus explains, "I needed clothes and you clothed me, I was sick and you looked after me, I was in prison and you came to visit me" (Matthew 25:36). This is how we keep the fire alive: By doing things for one another, we are actually doing things for God.

So how can we reconcile our faith with everyday living? How can we make this chapter practical for our lives? While it is powerful to read about the lives of others, the power is lost if we do not know how to make an application to our lives. So how can we learn to focus on the journey of our relationship? I'd like to challenge you to take the following steps in your relationship with God:

1. Chart Out Your Relationship With God

Look at where the ebbs and flows occur. I have done a lot of self-revelation in this book so far, and I can honestly tell you that I tend to slowly let God's hand go when I have a new love in my life. During those times I must consciously make an effort to spend time with God. I imagine this is how Gomer felt. Like a blue jay, she was distracted by every shiny thing. Every new man who passed her by and gave her attention temporarily made her forget she had a man at home. If we recognize our tendency to let God go at certain times, it'll be easier for us to look for the signs of these distractions and spot them while they are still looming on the horizon.

What is it in your life that makes you let go of the hand of God?

2. Be Intimate With God

Have you ever thought of why marriage relationships are so powerful when they're successful and so painful when they fail? I would suggest it's because of the level of intimacy it entails. I once heard someone give the illustration that the bond created by having sex with someone is like gluing two pieces of paper together. Now let me take it one step further and suggest that it's like gluing two pieces of different-colored construction paper together. Imagine that you have two sheets of it: One is white, and the other is red. Imagine spreading a thick glob of Elmer's glue on the red sheet of paper. Now slap the white piece of paper on the red and press the two together. Imagine letting the glue dry and trying to tear the two pieces apart from one another. Inevitably, remnants of one sheet will be attached to the other; patches of red will be forever stuck on the white, and vice versa. Intimacy is a good thing in a relationship—a great thing, even. Without it the relationship would not survive.

In order to keep the fire alive with God, we must maintain our intimacy with Him. We must be willing to expose ourselves "naked" to Christ, as in showing our vulnerabilities, faults, and flaws to Him. In the case of Adam and Eve, it is possible to explain this concept literally *and* figuratively. Prior to sinning, Adam and Eve had no problem exposing themselves to God. As it says in Genesis 2:25, they didn't even realize they were naked: "Adam and his wife were both naked, and they felt no shame." In contrast, after they sinned, they wanted to wait until they were fully clothed to stand before God. "Then the eyes of both of them were opened, and they realized they were naked; so they sewed fig leaves together and made coverings for themselves" (Genesis 3:7).

This desire to cover themselves before coming to God decreased their ability to be intimate with Him. When we let God see all of our imperfections, we are ready to become intimate with Him. Intimacy is preceded by vulnerability. It's about admitting and letting Him deal with our struggles. It is through this true intimacy that we are able to keep the fire alive.

3. Continue to Date

Dating is our personal time spent with Christ. To keep the fire alive, we must continue to get to know Him and allow Him to know us intimately. How do we date God? Simply put, through our devotional lives. When we are interested in someone, we usually set aside quality time. The same is true for God. However, we will not benefit from "dating God" if we are not in the mind-set for relationship building. In the story of the Samaritan woman, her encounter with Jesus was successful because she was open to building a relationship with Him. He already knew her faults and flaws, but she showed Him her willingness to build a relationship when she accepted His show of affection and admitted her vulnerabilities.

Typically when we date, we decide what cards we'll put on the table. We chose those that will represent us in the best light. When dating Jesus, we must place *all* of our cards on the table. We must be willing to be exposed before Him and have an open mind to get to know Him. Here are some ways to put this into action:

Create a Devotional Plan.

Before setting out to study, come up with a plan. For instance, make a decision to read a chapter of the gospels each day while listening to *The Bible Experience*. Try reading the Crucifixion story each day, which can be found in Matthew 27, Mark 15, Luke 23, and John 19, to gain a better appreciation for Jesus' sacrifice for us. Or you may decide to read the Bible through in a year. Whatever you decide to do, remember that having a plan up front will give you some direction in your study.

Set Aside a Time to Meet Up With God

Set aside a special time each day that is reserved for you and God. Be fastidious about keeping your date with Him. When you make an effort through your time, you will also make an effort through your actions as well.

Talk and Listen Through Prayer

In your devotional life, make sure to set aside time to pray and listen to God. Speak with Him openly as if you were talking to a friend. Be vulnerable in front of Him. When you are honest with Him about where you are, He can more easily take you where He wants you to be.

4. Do Special Things for Him

In relationships, gifts are a great way for us to express our love. Within our relationship with God, our gifts are our selves and our actions. We don't do things for Christ to receive our salvation; instead they are an expression of our love. John 14:15 says, "If you love me, keep my commands." As we discussed in chapter 5 on praise, we are neither rewarded nor punished as we deserve. So our gifts to God are an expression of love for what He has already done for us. In order to keep the fire alive, we must in turn do special things for God, showing our love in the same way we show our faith: "As the body without the spirit is dead, so faith without deeds is dead" (James 2:26).

So what can we do for God? Jesus answers this question in Matthew 25:40 when He said, "Whatever you did for one of the least of these brothers and sisters of mine, you did for me." So join an outreach group. Care for those around you. Look for the face of Jesus in everyone. Search for ways you can do something special for others, because you're really doing it for Him. But we can't act out of order. You can't easily do something special for Him if you don't know Him. "Not everyone who says to me, 'Lord, Lord,' will enter the kingdom of heaven, but only the one who does the will of my Father who is in heaven. Many will say to me on that day, 'Lord, Lord, did we not prophesy in your name, and in your name drive out demons and in your name perform many miracles!' Then I will tell them plainly, 'I never knew you. Away from me, you evildoers!'" (Matthew 7:21-23).

So in our effort to keep the fire alive, it's important to do special things for God. But remember that this expression of love is an overflow of the love we already have in our relationship with Him.

5. Receive His Constructive Criticism

We can't stay in God's presence and continue to be the same. We must change. We can't continue to embrace our old habits and our old way of doing things (and we will speak on this topic in greater depth in chapter 8, on sin). But remember, in order to keep the fire alive, we must accept God's constructive criticism for our lives that we find in His Word.

6. Don't Be Ashamed of Your Relationship With Him

Don't be ashamed to talk about Him, but more important, don't be afraid to *show* Him. Think back to the story of Gomer: if she had been more free in acknowledging her relationship with Hosea with those she encountered, I'm sure she would have avoided many of her problems. People must know your status. They must know that you are in a relationship with God—a meaningful relationship that you are unwilling to compromise.

For some, when the music plays at the end of a pastor's compelling sermon, it is easier to be drawn to the front and commit to a new life in Christ. But sometimes after we arrive at the familiarity of home, the new car smell wears off, and once again the relationship with God is denied its place as first priority. This is modern-day Gomer syndrome.

So how can I remain faithful after the feeling of new love has worn off? How can I continue to want God? I've discovered that it's hard to keep a relationship alive when one's heart's not in it. Couch potato Christians are not Christians for long, and God asks us to be faithful to Him throughout the journey. So I ask myself every time I fall, *What's my excuse?* God has already piqued my curiosity, so I must continue to work to keep the fire alive. If I put in the effort on my end, God will surely and powerfully reciprocate.

Sex, Drugs, and Rock and Roll

The Sin Factor:
The Story of Adam and Eve

had seen him there before, bent in a most uncomfortable position. Knees folded like a praying mantis, face to the floor, arms extended in front of him with a beat-up baseball cap in his hands. While being in the city sometimes desensitizes you to the familiar faces of the homeless that grace the corners and bridges, this prostrated figure etched itself in my mind. It's very seldom you see a homeless man in Chicago plead with the public in such a humiliating way. Though I had passed him before, that day something tugged at my heart to act. I saw many people pass him by, some without even a glance. I was a little self-conscious about approaching him in my business casual; if I wanted to, I could easily just blend into the populace as I looked like any other young professional on a lunch break.

He didn't see me coming as his head was down, limiting his view to the pavement directly in front of him. After dropping $2 into his hat, I touched him lightly on the shoulder and asked, "Why are you knelt down, love?"

He glanced in the hat at what I had given him, then quickly looked back down and responded, "I just need a few more dollars to get something to eat." I asked his name. He said Barry; then as a farewell he added, "Pray for me."

I said, "OK," and walked away.

After about 10 steps it struck me. He asked for prayer. Perhaps I could be part of an answer. I returned and asked what he wanted to eat. He asked for a Big Mac and something to drink. I walked a block away, ordered the food, and made my return. As I awkwardly carried the bag of food and he saw me coming, I could see him rising from his knees to receive the meal. Then it occurred to me: I *wanted*, more than anything else, for Barry to rise from his knees.

That's what Jesus wants from us. He knows that because of sin our vision has become so skewed that we've lost perspective, as if we're just staring at the ground. We're on our knees, begging the world for things of little value, and in doing that, we devalue things that have tremendous worth. We spend our entire lives chasing money and fame in various forms. Jesus tries endlessly to give us perfection through gifts with immeasurable worth, but we continue to settle for "good enough." We are satisfied with the scraps and leftovers of this world, and oftentimes we're willing to do most anything to get them. Jesus came that He might restore our dignity, get us off of our knees, and stop us from begging the world for spare change.

Let me explain. Jesus says, "I have come that they may have life, and have it to the full" (John 10:10). But sin has paralyzed us from fully participating in life as God intended. Sin has infected us with a selfishness that is embarrassing when we think of it. Sin has stolen wealth and given the world poverty in its place, robbing parents of the ability to feed their families. Sin has stolen peace and given the world war, robbing countries of its young and able. Sin has stolen generosity and given the world selfishness in its place, robbing the world of truly connecting with one another. Sin has stolen good health and given the world sickness, diseases, and death. Imagine a father unable to feed his family because of poverty. Imagine a person having to beg for some extra coins just to eat one night. Sin has crippled humanity in such a way that it has robbed all of us. And only Jesus can lift us off of our knees and restore our dignity.

Sin has some of its biggest effects on our relationships. In fact, when thinking over some of my friendships, I realize that I have a deep personality flaw: I avoid awkward conversations. I remember the time I knew I would most likely miss my friend's wedding because of a prior obligation. When she texted me to ask if I planned to come, I turned the situation over a thousand ways in my mind to see if I could make it, but her wedding was a two-hour plane trip from my prior obligation. I avoided letting her know I probably wouldn't make it, and even worse, I avoided, after the wedding was over, explaining why I hadn't made it. A year of awkward silence passed between us before I finally reached out to right my wrong.

Though that situation was not particularly grievous, it created an awkward space in our friendship. At the time the incident was a small mistake; but because I waited to address the issue, something that was initially small created a chasm in our friendship.

Unfortunately I have carried this behavior into my relationship with God. I often avoid awkward conversations with Him as well. Several weeks before I wrote this chapter a number of my morning devotions dealt with the topic of sin. At the time, I was praying about something different, and I kept thinking to myself, *I wish God would talk to me.* Little did I realize that He was doing just that—the only problem was that He was bringing up a topic I didn't want to discuss.

For me this conversation had all the awkwardness of a father-daughter talk about the birds and the bees. I had little to say, and everything He shared seemed to make me squirm uncomfortably. But it's not awkward for Him, as He deals with sin all the time. Each time He brought it up, though, I would quickly scan through the devotion and say to myself, *This one isn't speaking to my situation; I haven't done anything wrong.*

Perhaps this explains why I had the hardest time writing this chapter. Perhaps it's because I had to admit I had a problem, and it's part of human nature to avoid responsibility. I never said it out loud, but somehow in the back of my mind I thought sin was a *you*-but-not-*me* type of problem. As bad as it sounds, I honestly didn't feel like I had done anything that was *too* bad. I've tried to live a fairly just and moral life. I give money in church and try to help those around me. But then I realized that the more comfortable I become with this idea, the more I am in danger. That means that I am comfortably blind to the sin in my life, which makes me comfortably blind to my need for a Savior. And I think this is where many of us are. We can't perceive our need for a Savior because we don't really think we have a problem. Our God gauge is off.

Sin is like any other addiction—the hardest part is getting us to admit we have a problem. Fortunately Jesus knew beforehand how hard it would be for humans to "man up" and take responsibility, so He spoke in terms of our physical needs to help us to conceptualize our spiritual need of Him.

Have you ever fasted, or simply gone a long time without eating? Have you ever been in the midst of a long bout of exercise without water? At one point I was training for a half marathon in Chicago and went for long runs every Sunday morning. One Sunday I got outside a bit later than normal, which caused it to be hotter than I was used to. I ran about three miles until I reached Navy Pier, and it wasn't until then that I realized I was dehydrated.

At first I began to casually look for a water fountain, thinking I would happen upon one. But as I continued running, my search became more frantic. I could feel my skin tingle, and tiny goose bumps began to pop up everywhere. I didn't have money, so getting drinking water depended on me finding a free water fountain (or begging someone for spare change). Finally I found one, only to discover the water pressure was very low and the water wasn't coming out high enough for me to drink. I continued my search. By this time I began to think I was seeing mirages of oases in the glass and steel desert of the city. My run had degenerated into a slow crawl. I was desperate for a drink.

Sometimes God has to physically bring us to this place so that spiritually we understand our need for Him. We studied the story of the Samaritan woman in chapter 3, regarding our relationship with God, but I believe God has another lesson to teach us here as well—and it digs deeper into our need for Him. In John 4:7 we see Jesus asking the Samaritan woman if she would give *Him* a drink of water. This one question sparks a lively conversation between the two of them. What's even more interesting is the analogy Jesus gives the woman to help her conceptualize her need of Him. He says, "Everyone who drinks this water will be thirsty again, but whoever drinks the water I give them will never thirst. Indeed, the water I give them will become in them a spring of water welling up to eternal life" (John 4:13, 14). In this conversation Jesus is helping the woman prioritize her needs into primary and secondary categories. She was already aware of her physical need, as she was at the well to draw water for her household. Jesus capitalized on that secondary (physical) need to explain her primary (spiritual) need for something that was less tangible, but much more important.

And every drink needs a good meal, so to ensure readers would fully understand, Jesus continued on. The disciples saw Jesus with the Samaritan woman and though they were surprised, they didn't say anything. They had left Jesus to get something to eat, so naturally upon their return, they urged Jesus to eat something. At this Jesus replied, "I have food to eat that you know nothing about." "My food is to do the will of him who sent me and to finish his work" (verses 32, 34).

I find it fascinating that in two instances, in the same chapter of John, we see Jesus using our physical needs of food and drink to explain our spiritual need of Him. Because sin has caused our God gauge to be skewed, it is easy to think we can go a day without God, but when we put it into the context of our physical needs, it's much easier to understand that spiritually, we must yearn for God as we would for our daily food and water.

Unfortunately, within the human story is a general unawareness of the state we're in and a lack of understanding of our need. I often walk down the street and hurt for humanity. I hurt for the point of suffering we have collectively reached. What's sadder still is that we don't realize we've been knocked down to our knees, begging the world for its scraps. But then, things usually don't make sense until we understand them in context.

One of my favorite scenes from *The Fresh Prince of Bel-Air* is Geoffry, the butler, feeding conflicting stories to the various family members, causing them to fly into frenzies. As they all go running out of the room, Geoffry remains with a sly look on his face, lifts his hands, rocks them back and forth like a puppeteer, and says mockingly, "Dance, puppets, dance!" And while it's amusing to watch on TV, it's not so amusing when we realize we're the ones being yanked around—*we* are the puppets. While few of us realize it, we are part of a story that stretches far beyond our birth, with a plot much deeper than what we'll eat tonight for dinner, how much we'll make this year, or what career we'll pursue.

The concept of a cosmic battle between good and evil is not far-fetched. We frequently consume it in movies, TV series, toys, costumes, and other paraphernalia. Yet somehow it's more comfortable for the human mind to accept the subject as fantasy than reality. Since childhood days of playing cops and robbers we have accepted the concept of good against evil. All of these stories told on the big screen are really a reflection of the bigger story that's happening right in front of us.

No matter how comfortable your life is, no matter how much your job pays, no matter how excited your kids are to see you when you get home or how loving your significant other is, there always seems to be something that is "off." There is always something to worry about. Tragedies happen to unsuspecting people. People with life and vibrancy unexpectedly die. Horrific natural disasters strike and people exhibit unfathomable behavior. While you can't quite put your finger on the cause, you know something's off. It's as though you return to your house in the evening only to find everything in a different place than where you left it—something is not quite right. And inevitably the biggest question of all that plagues the minds of humans is what happens when we die. As human beings we've stepped out of the order of things as they were meant to be.

Let's take a look back. Imagine Eve sitting on the dew-dampened grass like a crumpled piece of paper, Abel's lifeless head lying limply in her lap. She looks up where Cain had been standing when he had recounted the story to her, his face hardening with each passing moment. A wave of emotions washes over her, each one so unfamiliar at that point. Though many things had changed since that fateful day in the garden, never in her wildest imagination could she have conceived of this. She glances again where Cain had been standing and grapples with his explanation, but can't bring herself to recount the details of how her son had met his untimely death at the hands of his brother. Out of all the emotions that flood her, guilt rises to the top. If she disallowed herself from feeling anything else, she would permit herself to feel guilt. She deserved it, after all.

As she traces the outline of young Abel's face, a slideshow of memories flashes through her mind. They come faster than ever before, and while she works hard to make their colors fade, she can't fight the vibrancy. They feel as weighty as Abel's head feels in her lap. While all the other memories speed by, one seems to crawl at a snail's pace, almost in defiance: the image of the serpent. Even in memory it is mesmerizing.

She remembers the exact place she had been standing in the garden. Just the thought conjures up memories of the strong scent of jasmine and the shock of colors of the trees and flowers, each one clamoring for her attention. There was always something new to learn and discover in the garden. It was as if God were playing a game of treasure hunt. She remembers how Adam took such joy in introducing her to all the animals he had named and sharing their unique qualities with her. Eve loved Adam for his wealth of knowledge. She not only felt wrapped in an enormous blanket of love while she was in his presence—she also felt as though she was learning so much. And she sensed that what he loved about her was her curious spirit and loquaciousness. Eve had a question about everything and always wanted to know how things worked. She filled the air with the melody of her words, and Adam seemed to wallow in it a like a happy piglet wallows in a puddle of mud without a care in the world.

As she thinks back, she realizes it was most likely her curiosity that lured her away that day. She found herself admiring some of the vegetation in a section of the garden to which she didn't often venture. At the time, she was fascinated with the *Mimosa pudica* plant, also known as the shy plant. She watched in amusement as the leaves reacted to her touch. With a gentle brush of her fingers on the leaves they immediately respond by shyly folding their two sides together. Just as she touched the third set of leaves she heard a voice behind her that had the gentle tinkle of the sound of a harp.

"Did God really say, 'You must not eat from any tree in the garden'?" (Genesis 3:1).

Eve whipped around quickly, looking for the source of the voice. She spotted it—the most mesmerizing thing she had ever seen. In every way it captured her attention, and the sound of the creature's voice was in every way engaging. Eve struggled to gain her composure and make her tongue function, as she was so taken aback. "Ahem," she cleared her throat. "We may eat fruit from the trees in the garden, but God did say, 'You must not eat fruit from the tree that is in the middle of the garden, and you must not touch it, or you will die'" (verse 2).

A glint of disbelief crossed the eyes of the serpent. In that moment it almost shined brighter and seemed more inviting. "'You will not surely die,' the serpent said. . . . 'For God knows that when you eat from it your eyes will be opened, and you will be like God, knowing good and evil'" (verses 4, 5).

Eve quickly shakes the thought from her mind. Her heart starts to feel dense, as though it can hardly stand to hold its own weight and continue beating. Abel's head is impossibly heavy as it rests in her lap. She begins to sob so loudly that soon Adam finds her there. In an instant his eyes sweep the scene and he immediately knows what has taken place, though he doesn't understand why. He collapses next to Eve, embracing her and joining in her sorrow. Eve begins to tremble, and her wailing succumbs to a muffled chant: "This is all my fault! This is all my fault! I killed my son! This is all my fault!" Adam tries to console her, but in that moment there is no dam strong enough to hold back the flood of emotions.

As Adam sits there with his family in his arms, he too is taken back to that fateful day. He remembers it with an electrical charge in the air, as though the earth knew something Adam did not. Looking back, he realizes that he and Eve did not understand their lives in context.

When they hid in shame at the sound of God's voice, Adam immediately knew that something had changed in their relationship. This had always been their favorite time of day, but that day a heavy sense of embarrassment hung in the air. After "finding" them, God managed to pull the story from His creations, who stood shamefully before Him. At this moment of reckoning, each pointed blame at the other. When they finished, God spoke in a very even tone. His pronouncement was said with the heavy consequence of a judge and the sorrow of a mother nursing her young child's cut after a big fall.

It was hearing the consequences and sensing God's disappointment that crushed Adam the most. Though he hadn't purposely memorized the words, somehow he couldn't seem to forget them: first the fate of the creature, then the fate of humanity.

"Because you have done this, cursed are you above all livestock and all wild animals! You will crawl on your belly and you will eat dust all the days of your life. And I will put enmity between you and the woman, and between your offspring and hers; he will crush your head, and you will strike his heel" (verses 14, 15).

Adam shakes his head in disbelief. He shares Eve's feeling of guilt for the murder of their son. With the deepest remorse he wonders how he could have disobeyed God's direct command, as though he had a better way, as though he somehow knew more than his Creator. He had never imagined his action would one day cause him to have to hold his murdered son in his arms.

Though he had seen the consequences of sin before, in his work for the family's food and in the sacrifices they now offered, never had the consequences so directly touched his family and his heart. Now he is certain there is an invisible battle raging, just as God had explained.

After that day in the garden, God no longer came "in person" for their evening talks as He once did. His absence was a gaping hole in their family. But still He spoke plainly to Adam and Eve about the great controversy. He told them the story of the most beautiful creature He had ever created. He explained that he was "the seal of perfection, full of wisdom and perfect in beauty" (Ezekiel 28:12). Both Adam and Eve could attest to his beauty, as they had seen the mesmerizing creature, albeit as a serpent and not in his natural form.

God told the story with so much sorrow that it was as though a cello wailed out a dirge in accompaniment. As He spoke, it was obvious to Adam and Eve that the beauty and talent God had given the creature as a gift had become his biggest downfall. Adam and Eve sat in rapt attention as God explained to them the conflict that ensued in heaven. In the same way the creature had tricked Adam and Eve, he had also tricked one third of the angels in heaven into believing God was someone He was not. God explained, "Then war broke out in heaven. Michael and his angels fought against the dragon, and the dragon and his angels fought back. But he was not strong enough, and they lost their place in heaven. The great dragon was hurled down—that ancient serpent called the devil, or Satan, who leads the whole world astray. He was hurled to the earth, and his angels with him" (Revelation 12:7-9). And in hearing this, Adam and Eve learned that the common thread, both in the story of the deceitful creature and in their world, was selfishness.

Though neither will speak, both know the other is also recounting God's words. They sit in silence with their lifeless son in their arms. All they can think of is their decision, in context, now affecting the whole earth and everyone who would come after them.

Just like Adam and Eve, we must put our lives into context. We must realize that in the background of our lives runs a story with a deeper plot than our day-to-day activities. In our own struggles we must learn that "we wrestle not against flesh and blood but against principalities, against powers, against the rulers of the darkness of this world, against spiritual wickedness in high places" (Ephesians 6:12, KJV). This will teach us to put our lives into context.

The framework of the story is that individually we each have a sin problem that is part of a bigger problem, which creates an enormous gap in our relationship with God. Until recently I didn't understand the connection between my prayers and my sin. But a verse in Isaiah has provided me insight: "But your iniquities have made a separation between you and your God, and your sins have hidden His face from you so that He does not hear" (Isaiah 59:2, NASB).

A first read of the verse makes it sound pretty judgmental, almost suggesting that I can never approach God in prayer. But upon careful study I realize that through this verse God is giving me a key to relationship building. Previously, when God didn't immediately answer a prayer request, it caused a stalemate in our relationship. However, as I have begun to understand the effect of sin in our relationship, I have a better understanding of His character. As we learned in the chapter on prayer, Matthew 6:33 teaches us to "seek first his kingdom and his righteousness, and all these things will be given to you as well." I realized that in expecting an answer to my prayer *before* allowing God to deal with my sin problem, I was asking God to address a secondary need when He had not yet dealt with my primary problem—my lack of acknowledgment of sin and the awkward space it creates in my relationship with Him.

In the moment of realizing that, I felt like Eve: naked, ashamed, and embarrassed. I realized I had made a series of small decisions that had pushed me away from God. None of them were big, none of them were what people would call "bad," but still they had created this awkward space between us. And even worse, they had caused me to misrepresent Him.

Have you ever realized that you may be the only picture of Christ that someone may see? I used to wince at the verse that says, "My son, do not make light of the Lord's discipline, and do not lose heart when he rebukes you, because the Lord disciplines the one he loves, and he chastens everyone he accepts as his son" (Hebrews 12:5, 6). But now I get it. Because we are a reflection of God, He cannot allow us to show an inaccurate picture of who He is. When I thought about this in the context of my relationship with my boss, it scared me. One day I felt so bothered about the way I had behaved in our interactions that I asked if we could meet. During the meeting we chatted about work and our relationship. We shared helpful insights with one another. But the part that still sticks out in my mind is her sharing with me my areas that needed improvement. As I listened intently, I realized I had heard those words before in other situations, at other jobs, from my parents, and from friends. I thought to myself that perhaps this wasn't my boss speaking. Maybe through this series of experiences, God is trying to tell me something about my character. So instead of chalking my actions up to my personality and leaving it at that, I realized God was tapping me on the shoulder, trying to get me to acknowledge my behavior, and that completely changed my perspective. This put me in the perfect place for relationship building. I was finally ready to admit that I have a problem, thereby acknowledging my desperate need for a Savior. And everyone loves a good rescue story.

I stopped in my tracks one morning while watching *Good Morning America*. I was drawn into hearing the most unlikely rescue story of a grandmother in Texas who was abducted from her home at gunpoint by an 18-year-old criminal and dragged across town to an 18-foot-deep cistern. The woman was given three choices on her fate: The young, hardened criminal would either strangle her, shoot her, or toss her down the well. Before the frightened grandmother could give her response, she found herself being thrown down this dark, dank hole where she landed in a pool of stagnant water. She periodically screamed out and prayed, afraid that she would meet her death in that hole.

Her family went by her house a few times before realizing that the she was missing and obviously in trouble. The telling clue ended up being a message left on her cell phone from the police, who had caught the perpetrator joyriding in her car. The family quickly went into action, searching for their missing loved one. Suddenly a thought crossed the son's mind, and though highly unlikely, the family quickly set out to pursue the hunch to search for his mother in the local well. Upon arrival they called down the well, and immediately she responded. After waiting for more than 16 hours, her help finally arrived.

We too are in desperate need of a Savior. Whether we have admitted it or not, we suffer from the problem of sin, which has selfishness at its root. If you feel totally unworthy of God's love, you're in the perfect place for relationship building.

While we discussed how sin entered the earth, I'm grateful the story doesn't end there. Whenever you feel overwhelmed, thrown to the ground, and drowning in your sins, visit Psalm 103 and Matthew 27. I guarantee they will give you assurance of the love of the Savior.

If you have not yet humbly approached the throne of God, asking for forgiveness of your sins, I invite you to read 1 John 1:9: "If we confess our sins, He is faithful and righteous to forgive us our sins and to cleanse us from all unrighteousness" (NASB) and pray this simple prayer of faith:

Heavenly Father, You tell us in Psalm 103:10-14 that "he does not treat us as our sins deserve or repay us according to our iniquities. For as high as the heavens are above the earth, so great is his love for those who fear him; as far as the east is from the west, so far has he removed our transgressions from us. As a father has compassion on his children, so the Lord has compassion on those who fear him; for he knows how we are formed, he remembers that we are dust." So, Lord, in the name of Jesus I am coming before You asking for Your forgiveness of my sins. I pray that You will help me lead the life that You've planned for me—one that represents You. In Jesus' name, amen.

As we begin to address the problem of sin in our lives, we make things ready for God to find the perfect accommodations in our lives.

A Place to Call Home

The Body as a Sanctuary:
The Story of the Sanctuary

Arriving at the home of my friend's family in London after trekking around Europe was a welcomed respite from sleeping in the straight-back commuter seats offered by the train and the unforgiving bunk beds in hostels. Many a night, after exploring the gems of France, Italy, Belgium, the Netherlands, and Germany, we tucked ourselves neatly into the width of a train's bench and rested our heads in the crook of a book bag doubling as a pillow. We found that spending the night in the safe confines of the train would save us €20 that could be used for the next day's meals. Because we were coming from accommodations that were less than ideal, I was more than excited to be in England, a foreign country that promised to be more familiar. Almost as exciting as the prospect of a comfortable bed was the fact that everyone in this country spoke my language, albeit with a strange accent. The signs were in English, the TV belted out its shows in English and most important, the people on the streets spoke English.

Despite all our plans to explore England, we did more resting than touring. On one of the days we did venture out, I remember more of the moment we arrived home than what we saw that day. Upon entering the house, we were greeted by the hearty smells of home cooking. My eyes landed on a meal fit for a hefty construction worker who had just arrived from a long day's labor. Although an ocean separated me from the familiar stars and stripes of my country's flag, it was in that place, at that moment, that I felt at home.

Many may wonder if a concept that's seemingly as antiquated as the sanctuary mentioned in the Bible is relevant to our lives today. They may ask what this intricate, portable building can teach us about relationship building with God. To answer that, we can look at the original purpose of the sanctuary in the desert, which was restoring relationships with God. The sanctuary has always been about closing the gap between God and men and creating a place where God can feel at home with us. In this chapter we will explore two sides of the sanctuary story; first we will examine the purpose of the service, then the role we play in this drama.

When Adam and Eve sinned, they stepped out of their face-to-face relationship with God. As we discussed in chapter 5 on praise, they essentially stopped acknowledging who God is. As a result, their relationship with God had to change. The way they interacted with Him changed. And this is apparent by the fact that they had to leave the Garden of Eden permanently (Genesis 3:24). However, because God's longing to still be in a relationship with them (and with us) was so strong and so deep, He had to be creative in His approach. He put into action a plan to restore the relationship with humankind. Exodus 29:42-46 reveals that God had Moses build the sanctuary so He could dwell among humankind: "'For the generations to come this burnt offering is to be made regularly at the entrance to the tent of meeting, before the Lord. There I will meet you and speak to you; there also I will meet with the Israelites, and the place will be consecrated by my glory. So I will consecrate the tent of meeting and the altar and will consecrate Aaron and his sons to serve me as priests. Then I will dwell among the Israelites and be their God. They will know that I am the Lord their God, who brought them out of Egypt so that I might dwell among them. I am the Lord their God.'"

But this was not enough. God was not satisfied with only a long-distance relationship with us; He longed to get things back to the way they used to be. But in order to do so, He had to deal with our sin problem. As we discussed in chapter 8, He had to get us up from our knees and restore our dignity, which is why we needed the plan of salvation (in which one died for many). As a result of this plan, we will no longer have to be in a long-distance relationship with God. We will once again be able to have a face-to-face relationship with Him (John 14:2, 3). But while its easy for us to look back and see the plan God had all along, the children of Israel struggled to see beyond the here and the now and truly fathom the plan of salvation. Spiritually, the children of Israel were just that—children. So like an elementary school teacher, God had to use very clear and simple examples to help them see His intentions.

Learning how to divide fractions is a milestone in any elementary school kid's academic career. My teacher was jovial and legendary; everyone knew him or at least knew of him. But he had a very distinct method of teaching students how to divide fractions. In order to divide fractions you must multiply by its reciprocal. To ensure there was no doubt what a reciprocal was, our teacher picked up one of the smaller guys in our class and more or less turned him upside down, all while explaining that a reciprocal is an upside-down fraction. We laughed and laughed as the blood rushed to our classmate's face and as he pretended to scream for mercy. It was an illustration that burned itself into our minds and forever served its purpose. I'm sure none of us will ever forget what a reciprocal is.

That's exactly what the sanctuary was for the children of Israel: a clear, simple and deep-seated example. This example for dividing fractions, however, did not solve a single math problem for us in itself. We never went to our classmate and turned him upside down again, because that example was just a shadow of the real thing. And so was the sanctuary. It never saved a single person by itself. It was simply preparing their hearts for the real thing.

After escaping the grips of slavery in Egypt, the children of Israel found themselves wandering around the vast expanse of desert in Sinai. Because they had been so far away from God for so long, God had to explain Himself and His character to them. Their God gauge was off. So instead of just telling them, God took every opportunity to show them, because this was His way of getting to their hearts most effectively. The washbasin, candlestick holder, incense, and ark of the covenant all had special meanings as they related to relationship building. But most important, the sacrifice of the lamb, done along with the confession of sins, had the greatest meaning of all.

Just as my eighth-grade teacher turned the student upside down as an illustration, the sanctuary was an illustration (or a shadow, as the Bible often calls it). And while the intricacies of the sanctuary were a marvel to behold, they failed to captivate anyone's attention in the same way as the actual sacrifice of the real Lamb of God. The killing of thousands of lambs over the course of many years failed to do what one Lamb did in one moment: take away the sins of the world.

The air pulsated with the buzz of the crowd. Indistinguishable sounds from all sides created a reverse theatric atmosphere—the action was on the hill, but nothing could be heard in the audience. Painted against the background of a diverse crowd of onlookers was the stark and powerful image of three crosses. While executions were common in the Roman Empire, on this day the primitive execution tools were noteworthy because they not only *suggested* the pain of death—they were exacting it.

Prior to dropping the crosses in their designated spots, those close to the action could hear the soldier let out a primal grunt with every strike of his hammer. The intensity of his shouts was matched only by the sound of the hammer hitting the nails that fixed Christ's body to the roughly hewn cross.

The two men on the crosses hanging to the left and the right let out cries of anguish. And then, as if somehow he were in the audience instead of onstage, one of the criminals was emboldened to join in with the crowd as they taunted Jesus, who hung in the middle.

"Aren't you the Messiah? Save yourself and us!" (Luke 23:39).

Suddenly, in the area that once reverberated with noise, there rested a cloud of silence which matched the darkness that hung over the area—just as a curtain falls between acts. Then like a knife cutting through the silence, Jesus, who had remained notably silent, called out "'Eloi, Eloi, lema sabachthani?' (which means 'My God, my God, why have you forsaken me?')" (Mark 15:34).

"The curtain of the temple was torn in two. Jesus called out with a loud voice, 'Father into your hands I commit my spirit.' When he had said this, he breathed his last" (Luke 23:45, 46).

Many of those present at the Crucifixion had also witnessed or participated in the sacrificial service in the sanctuary. They already had the harrowing task of slitting the innocent and unassuming lamb's throat as a part of confessing their sins. But they failed to see the connection between the two lambs. They were too blind to realize that everything was leading up to this moment. *This* was the climax of the story, but they were waiting for another ending. Had they paid attention to the signs, they would have realized that there had been a plethora of indicators.

There was so much foreshadowing this day. It had been explicitly spoken to them many times through the prophets and through the Scriptures. John the Baptist said it to them plainly before he baptized Jesus: "Look, the Lamb of God, who takes away the sin of the world" (John 1:29).

Jesus said in John 12:32, "And I, when I am lifted up from the earth, will draw all people to myself." He and His sacrifice are at the crux of this book. It is because of Jesus' sacrifice that we are even able to consider building a relationship with God, for "while we were still sinners, Christ died for us" (Romans 5:8).

That was the message Christ was trying to get across to the children of

Israel in the sanctuary, and that's the message He's still trying to get across to us. He is trying to recalibrate our God gauge. He is trying to put us in the perfect place for relationship building by closing the gap in our long-distance relationship.

The amazing part about our reconciliation with God is that even though the fluctuation of regression and progression in our relationship with Him is similar to that of a cheating spouse, He still wraps us in a bear hug and sees us through. Think about it: When a spouse cheats, they will most likely be kicked out of the house for a time. Then, once allowed back in, they will most likely make their bed on the pullout couch before they find themselves back in the room with their spouse. But this isn't God's idea of reconciliation at all. Although we're totally deserving of that type of treatment, God never treats us as we deserve. Instead of pushing us away, God tries to get as close to us as possible. He had used the earthly sanctuary to close the gap between God and humanity, but it served only as an example, pointing its participants to the real thing: Jesus' crucifixion and resurrection.

After His death on the cross, even the long-distance relationship He had reestablished with us wasn't good enough. But since there was no Temple structure, where would the Holy Spirit dwell? How would Jesus be able to continue to live among us? That's the exciting part *we* play in this drama. God wanted to be closer still, so He came to dwell *in* us. First Corinthians 6:19, 20 says, "Do you not know that your bodies are temples of the Holy Spirit, who is in you, whom you have received from God? You are not your own; you were bought at a price. Therefore honor God with your bodies."

So all this time God had been looking for creative ways to get as close to us as possible, and He found it in us. Have you created an inviting environment for Him to live in? Will He feel at home in your heart?

As I mentioned earlier, one of the times I felt the most at home was the time I was thousands of miles away from my country. This is because my hosts went out of their way to create a comfortable environment for me, from the food I ate to the bed I slept in to the conversation they made with me. How can we create a similarly comfortable environment for God in our hearts?

The most important aspect of the environment we create is the spiritual environment. No one stays in a place in which they're not welcome. We can easily create a type of spiritual environment in our lives where Jesus feels *un*welcome through the things we listen to, the things we read, and the things we watch. Oftentimes the ideas presented in these mediums can dull our appetites for God or confused our priorities. Have you created a comfortable place for God to live in your life in this area?

Emotionally we can create an environment that feels hostile for God. Harboring anger and an unforgiving spirit are like sleeping in a friend's house with two pit bulls staring you down as you try to fall asleep. These emotions can eat away at our core and tear away at our relationship not only with God, but also with those around us.

Another area that can make God feel unwelcome in our lives—one that often goes unnoticed—is our physical body. A friend once asked me why I eat the way I do. She explained that it was no longer necessary to follow the "eating regulations" as found in Leviticus. I myself have never eaten meat, and I began eating fish sometime in college (though I refrain from eating those fish whose job it is to clean the ocean, such as shellfish). I avoid alcohol and caffeinated products. I try to eat fruits and vegetables and drink as much water as I can each day, even though it can be a struggle for me at times. Basically, I try to treat my body as kindly as possible. And these practices were what she was referring to when she made the comment. I explained to her that God created the human body (Genesis 1:27)—therefore He knows best how to keep it functioning properly. Even car manufacturers have recommendations for the type of gas and oil that should be used in their vehicles. Is the human body any different?

The original diet that humans were given was one of fruits, grains, and nuts. Things did change after the Flood, when God gave permission to Noah and his family to use animals for food as well (Genesis 9), but even in this He placed regulations on what should and should not be eaten (Leviticus 11; Deuteronomy 14).

So how does this relate to relationship building? Well, if our body is the temple of God and He gave specific instructions to Moses on how to build and maintain the original sanctuary, isn't it likely that He has a plan for how He'd like us to maintain his new earthly temples (our bodies)?

Though we often miss it because of its intricate nature, the concept of the sanctuary—both the earthly structure and our bodies—is all about relationship building. It's about bridging the gap and transforming our long-distance relationship with God to a face-to-face one. Paying attention to these areas puts us in the perfect place for relationship building. Once we are in that perfect place, we will also be ideally set up to build relationships with one another, and for sharing an accurate picture of God with those around us.

What's Love Got to Do With It?

Relationship With Others:
The Story of Jacob and Esau

After submitting my letter of resignation for my first job, I was surprised to be called into the office for my exit interview. I guess they wanted to escort me out the same way they had welcomed me in—with a battery of questions. I noticed the same was true in a recent relationship. Among many other inquiries the inevitable question of why things didn't work out was asked. The answer I received was shocking and a little embarrassing: I didn't share my food. Obviously this couldn't be the primary reason the relationship ended, but it certainly was the funniest and gave me room for self-reflection. Let me explain.

My dining companion and I would often go out for dinner. In his overwhelming appetite he would scarf down his meal while I meticulously worked through my plate, savoring each bite along the way. Typically, about three fourths of the way through the meal I would be satisfied and ask the waiter for a take-out box, thinking that later in the day I would be hungry for the remainder of the meal. A little while after leaving the restaurant, my dining companion would begin to eye my take-out box and hint at his intentions of finishing off my leftovers. At the mention of these words, a wave of selfishness would take over me like a small child playing in the sandbox who hadn't quite learned to share. With this behavior of mine being brought to my attention, I got to thinking: If we had an exit interview at the end of life, what would people say about us and our relationships?

I had the chance to experience this when my maternal grandmother passed away. I was in my early 20s at the time, but I stayed close to the door of my mother's room, just as I had done when I was a small child. I hoped to catch a snippet of the conversation between her and my aunt as they recounted memories from my grandmother's life. I ended up learning lessons about her I never knew. Though she was quick to say what was on her mind, she also had compassion. I learned about the people's lives she'd touched. I heard stories about her interactions with others. It was almost like witnessing her exit interview. So I ask again: How do we want people to remember us after we are gone?

Reconciling Faith With Everyday Living

We are Christians, and our lives are love stories—or at least they should be. The theme of our lives should exhibit love in two key ways: the immense love we receive from God and the love we pass on to others. As you may have noticed, *Fish Food* is a book about relationship building and restoration with our Creator. But did you know that our relationships with others affect our relationship with God? In fact, unresolved issues in our earthly relationships can have a negative impact on our relationship with God. I know I had read 1 John 4:20 before, which says, "Whoever claims to love God yet hates his brother or sister is a liar. For whoever does not love their brother and sister, whom they have seen, cannot love God, whom they have not seen," but I didn't know how to reconcile my faith with my everyday living until I attended a prayer seminar hosted by a local church.

While many of the things the speaker said resonated with me, one principle stuck out more than any other—the need to forgive and reconcile our relationships. The speaker shared the biblical support for this as well as his own experience of doing it. That was enough to convince me. I felt convicted to go home and make a list of those whom I had offended and who had offended me. The following morning I sat down with my list and began to write letters. The theme of my morning was forgiveness.

While it was a humbling experience, it also gave me permission to let go. Some of the letters I wrote were to friends I had not spoken to in over a year. I got to thinking, *Why is reconciliation and relationship restoration so hard? Why is it so hard to forgive and ask for forgiveness?* Perhaps there is a lesson to be learned from the story of Jacob.

Gleaning from Genesis 25:19-28:11, we see Jacob fleeing his home-stead, along with a small bundle containing all of his possessions. His feet carried him forward, but his head continually glanced backward. Suspicion and fear swirled around him. In the same moment that he had won every-thing, he also felt as though he had lost it all.

He wished his shame would disappear, just as the sun slowly dipped over the edge of the horizon until it finally disappeared. As darkness settled in, Jacob set down his small bundle. Because he was hidden in the dark-ness, for the first time since his great deception he felt a sense of calm from external forces. Internally he was at war with his thoughts. Twice he had deceived his brother, successfully living up to the meaning of his name. The first time had been simple; he had only to take advantage of Esau's hunger. The second required a bit more conniving, a skill he seemed to be cultivating.

As he sat there in the darkness, he kept thinking of Esau. He was a man's man, and he had the chest hair to prove it. In fact, if hair were a requirement to prove manhood, Esau had long been a man, given that he popped out of his mother's womb covered in a blanket of hair. Esau also loved to be in the open field with his trusty bow and arrow, always on the hunt. Whenever he returned with his spoils, his father, Isaac, waited with bated breath to hear a play-by-play from the initial sighting of the kill until the final *hurrah*! Esau was always eager to share the gory details. Jacob, on the other hand, was much more nurturing and preferred to stick close to home, caring for the sheep. When he thought the boys weren't look-ing, Jacob sensed his father glancing at him and Esau, giving them each a quick once-over, trying to understand how they were conceived in the same womb at the same time. In his heart Jacob knew his mother, Rebekah, felt more at ease with him. Somehow he knew she understood him better; he just made more sense to her.

So on that fateful day, when Rebekah heard Isaac's feeble voice calling Esau to enter his tent because he had something important to say, she fol-lowed him with the stealth of a shadow, trailing close behind, always present but barely seen. An observer would have thought she was Esau's secretary the way she meticulously noted Isaac's instructions to Esau. As soon as Esau gathered his bow and arrows and headed out, Rebekah quickly ran to Jacob and shared all she had heard. With Rebekah as the ringleader, they began to scheme. Within seconds they had spun a web of deception in which Jacob gladly found himself caught. He quickly ran off to carry out his part.

Since her pregnancy, Rebekah knew there was something unusual about her boys. Although it was her first, the endless rounds of tussling that took place in her belly signaled she would have an interesting time parenting the pair. One evening, after barely catching a wink of sleep because of the endless jostling, she cried out to God for some sort of explanation of what was happening inside of her. God said to her, "Two nations are in your womb, and two peoples from within you will be separated; one people will be stronger than the other, and the older will serve the younger" (Genesis 25:23).

Rebekah contemplated these words as she stirred the pot that sat in front of her. The smell of fresh herbs and lamb's meat wafted from the cooking area to where Jacob found himself pacing back and forth. As he rehearsed what he would say to his father, his lips moved, but no sound came out. Not only did he want to steal his brother's blessing—he also wanted to avoid the inevitable curse he would receive from his father should he figure out what was going on.

Finally the meat was tender and seasoned as Isaac liked. Rebekah helped to outfit Jacob in the heavy animal skins he would have to wear to imitate his hairy brother. Though they were hot and itchy, Jacob knew this was a small price to pay for such a great reward. He sucked in a deep breath in an attempt to ease the tension within and to quiet the tiny voice that condemned his actions. When at last he had mustered the courage, he secured the pot containing the stew and prepared to enter his father's tent.

"My father . . ."

Isaac tilted his head in the direction of the sound.

"Yes, my son. Who is it?"

The voice Jacob tried on fit him like a mother's pair of high heels fits her young daughter. Though Jacob had practiced imitating Esau's voice all morning, it came out more like a squeak than the gruff manly sound he imagined. "I am Esau your firstborn. I have done as you told me. Please sit up and eat some of my game, so that you may give me your blessing" (Genesis 27:19).

He continued to try his best to disguise his voice, but every word that left his mouth etched another line of suspicion in Isaac's face.

"How did you find it so quickly, my son?" he asked. "The Lord your God gave me success," he replied (verse 20).

The conversation continued much like this, with lies baiting Isaac to give to Jacob that which rightfully belonged to Esau. After the blessing was finally given, just minutes after Jacob slipped out, the *real* Esau slipped in. His body was still jolted from the kill. His heart beat faster than normal in anticipation of his blessing. He entered Isaac's tent with words so strikingly similar to Jacob's, one would have thought they had read from the same script.

"'My father, sit up and eat some of my game, so that you may give me your blessing.' His father Isaac asked him, 'Who are you?' 'I am your son,' he answered, 'your firstborn, Esau.' Isaac trembled violently and said, 'Who was it, then, that hunted game and brought it to me? I ate it just before you came and I blessed him—and indeed he will be blessed'" (verses 31-33).

Those were the fatal words. That is why Jacob now found himself on the run. In his mind he had thought through *how* to steal the blessing, but he never let the situation play out beyond that moment. While the boys had many a brotherly scuffle growing up, he didn't know if their relationship could recover from this.

We began the story asking why it is so hard to forgive and ask for forgiveness. In my own experience, I have found that sometimes it's much easier to hang on than it is to let go. Some days, on the morning after an enormous sorrow, I find my mind searching furiously for the experience that bothered me the night before. It's as though my mind finds more comfort in holding on to pain than it does in releasing it. In the case of asking for forgiveness, it is often my pride and the pain of saying "I am wrong" that keeps me from doing it. Unfortunately, this attitude also keeps me from strengthening my relationship with God and from receiving His blessings. In one of the most common Bible passages, the Lord's Prayer, we see clear indication that we limit God's ability to forgive us when we fail to forgive others:

"Forgive us our debts, as we also have forgiven our debtors" (Matthew 6:12).

What a sobering thing to hear.

Delving back into Genesis, let's look at the events in chapters 31-33. It looks as though drama seemed to trail Jacob. Some of it was the inevitable kind that's bound to get anyone; the rest was the kind Jacob created. Long after escaping the drama with his brother, Jacob settled with his uncle (who also became his father-in-law) for quite some time. His one-man show had burgeoned into a huge production. Not only had Jacob's wealth increased, which was apparent by the herds of sheep, goats, camels and donkeys—he had also fathered 11 children. But after a while Jacob tired of living under the thumb of his father-in-law. So one day, with the stealth and strategy of a general, he decided to return to his homeland.

Just three days after the family began its clandestine escape, one of

Jacob's men came to share some harrowing news: his father-in-law, Laban, had been spotted close behind their caravan. In any normal family situation this would not cause concern, but Jacob knew if there was anyone sneakier than he was, it was Laban.

In fact, Laban was the only man he knew who could outtrick a trickster, and Jacob had the extra wife to prove it. The thought of his wedding was still bittersweet. From the day he had laid eyes on Rachel he was awestruck. Not only was she gorgeous—she was also captivating. He hated leaving her presence, because she energized him. Life somehow seemed brighter when she was around, and from the moment he stepped foot onto her father's land, everyone knew it—especially Laban. However, at that time Jacob was just a young man, owning not much besides the clothes on his back. He knew he could not yet rightfully ask for her hand in marriage. So Laban and Jacob agreed that Jacob would work seven years on Laban's land so that he could marry Rachel. The years went by quicker than he could have imagined. Looking back, it was a mystery how he didn't realize Laban's scheme at the time, but in his excitement and anticipation he was not aware enough to realize what was going on.

The morning after the wedding night, when he woke up to Leah instead of Rachel (realizing he didn't get what he paid for), Jacob screamed in fury, and within a hop, skip, and a jump he was at his father-in-law's tent. As soon as he looked at Laban, he saw the same glint in Laban's eyes he himself had given before—a glint of deception. A shouting match ensued that rivaled any animal battle ever seen in the wild. The negotiations weren't easy. You can't very well return a wife, so it was decided that Jacob would remain married to Leah, and Laban would give him Rachel as well—for an additional seven years of work. This was the kind of drama that trailed Jacob that he couldn't control.

When Laban caught up with them, he confronted Jacob for leaving without letting him know. Arguments and defenses flew back and forth. Finally, after a father-in-law/son-in-law heart-to-heart, the two straightened things out. Reconciliation had been made in their relationship, and now Jacob prepared for the next battle he would face with Esau. This was the drama he had brought on himself.

In comparison, his beef with Laban was like a schoolyard tussle. When it came to Esau, Jacob feared for his life, because Esau had every reason to want to kill him. Jacob had pulled off the biggest heist of that time. Before arriving at Esau's territory, Jacob sent messengers ahead of him to let Esau know he was on his way. In addition, Jacob tried to make it easier for Esau to forgive him by sending some gifts ahead of him. The response was intimidating. Esau was meeting Jacob with his crew of 400 men. After all, the past 20 years had made him a wealthy and powerful man.

Though Jacob didn't let on, fear shook him on the inside. He needed to be alone to pull his thoughts together. After sending his family ahead of him for the night, Jacob once again found himself enveloped in the darkness, but this time was markedly different. Before he was a young man with little life experience to his credit except for thievery. Now he had a family and had built a name for himself. In the midst of his thoughts, Jacob felt strong arms grip him. His instant reflex was to begin to struggle back. The darkness enshrouded the identity of the contender, and no words were exchanged during the struggle. Had Esau sent someone in the night to take him out silently, away from the eyes of his family? The fight between wills carried on for many hours until the sun threatened to reappear.

"When the man saw that he could not overpower him, he touched the socket of Jacob's hip so that his hip was wrenched as he wrestled with the man. Then the man said, 'Let me go, for it is daybreak.' But Jacob replied, 'I will not let you go unless you bless me.' The man asked him, 'What is your name?' 'Jacob,' he answered. Then the man said, 'Your name will no longer be Jacob, but Israel, because you have struggled with God and with humans and have overcome.' Jacob said, 'Please tell me your name.' But he replied, 'Why do you ask my name?' Then he blessed him there" (Genesis 32:25-29).

While there are many lessons to be learned from this story, the one that is the most relevant to our discussion is that God's blessing to Jacob came at the moment of his reconciliation with others—first with Laban and then with Esau. It was then that God had Jacob's attention. And God is concerned with our ability to forgive as well. Often He withholds our blessings until we have reconciled our relationships with others. The concept is similar to the one we discussed in chapter 8. God must deal with our primary problem of sin before He can deal with the secondary problem of our temporal needs.

When Jesus was on earth, He was asked the greatest commandment. "Jesus replied: 'Love the Lord your God with all your heart and with all your soul and with all your mind.' This is the first and greatest commandment. And the second is like it: 'Love your neighbor as yourself.' All the Law and the Prophets hang on these two commandments" (Matthew 22:37-40).

God's love is best exemplified through our relationships with one another. He not only wants to be in a loving relationship with us—He also wants us to be in loving relationships with one another as well.

Throughout my life I have had four moms. Before you deem this a biological impossibility, let me explain. Growing up, I had a Mexican mom, an Indian mom, a Dominican mom, and my diva African-American mom. Being surrounded by so many godly women taught me a lot about relationships.

I knew my Indian mom from church. I often ate Sabbath meals at her house and spent time with her sons, who are much younger than me. As ridiculous as it sounds, while in grade school I asked my parents if I could live with her family during the week and return home on the weekends because I enjoyed being at her house so much. Besides teaching me how to enjoy spicy Indian food, she taught me about loving and being loved. She adored me because she had two boys and had always wanted a girl. I cherish the lessons I learned from her about love.

My Dominican mom is the wife of the pastor I had growing up. She was also surrounded by men (her husband and three sons), and this, I believe, was one of the primary reasons she took me into her family. She always saw my potential and encouraged me in everything I did. I cherish the lessons I learned from her about mentorship.

By the time I went to boarding academy for high school I lived far away from all of my "moms," and it was then that I met my Mexican mom. She was the academy's registrar, and I took an enormous liking to her. Sometimes I spent the weekend over at her house, making crafts and filling up on home-cooked meals. When my high school boyfriend moved away, she brought me food and always checked in to make sure I was hanging in there. I'll never forget her show of love. I cherish the lessons I learned from her about compassion.

My diva African-American mom is the one I most aspire to be like. I almost fear the day when I become a mother, because I'm afraid I won't be able to measure up to what she is to me. She's taught me all I need to know about love, patience, and potential. To her, I've never had a crazy idea. Each one has had potential. But truth be told, I've come up with some outrageous things, and nonetheless she's always been more than encouraging. I cherish the lessons I learned from her about potential.

While I learned many lessons about love, compassion, mentorship, and potential from these women, I am by no means a master at building relationships. In my first year of college I was voted the shyest girl in the class, which in my opinion was a paradox. If the students knew to vote for me, I must not have been *that* shy. Therefore, in my mind I somehow managed to steal the title from some more deserving girl.

Now in my adult life, it's been indicated on Facebook that one of my weaknesses is that I'm not talkative. While this is the opinion of the people, I believe this is a problem of perception. An independent spirit is one of my greatest and worst qualities. Throughout life I have often been comfortable rolling solo. I am typically fine with going against the grain and being the only one making a particular decision. But it's also because of this independent spirit that sometimes God is unable to connect with me.

A careful analysis of the Ten Commandments reveals that God is genuinely concerned with our relationships with others. The first four set boundaries in and focus on our relationship with God while the last six set boundaries in and focus on our relationship with one another. Let's look at Exodus 20:3-17:

1. "You shall have no other gods before me.
2. "You shall not make for yourself an image in the form of anything in heaven above or on the earth beneath or in the waters below. You shall not bow down to them or worship them; for I, the Lord your God, am a jealous God, punishing the children for the sin of the parents to the third and fourth generation of those who hate me, but showing love to a thousand generations of those who love me and keep my commandments.
3. "You shall not misuse the name of the Lord your God, for the Lord will not hold anyone guiltless who misuses his name.
4. "Remember the Sabbath day by keeping it holy. Six days you shall labor and do all your work, but the seventh day is a Sabbath to the Lord your God. On it you shall not do any work, neither you, nor your son or daughter, nor your male or female servant, nor your animals, nor any foreigner residing in your towns. For in six days the Lord made the heavens and the earth, the sea, and all that is in them, but he rested on the seventh day. Therefore the Lord blessed the Sabbath day and made it holy.
5. "Honor your father and your mother, so that you may live long in the land the Lord your God is giving you.
6. "You shall not murder.
7. "You shall not commit adultery.

8. "You shall not steal.
9. "You shall not give false testimony against your neighbor.
10. "You shall not covet your neighbor's house. You shall not covet your neighbor's wife, or his male or female servant, his ox or donkey, or anything that belongs to your neighbor."

In the New Testament, Jesus delves even further into the last six, presenting something radically different from what our natural instinct prompts us to do. During one sermon He said, "You have heard that it was said, 'Love your neighbor and hate your enemy.' But I tell you, love your enemies and pray for those who persecute you, that you may be children of your Father in heaven. He causes his sun to rise on the evil and the good, and sends rain on the righteous and the unrighteous. If you love those who love you, what reward will you get? Are not even the tax collectors doing that? And if you greet only your people, what are you doing more than others? Do not even pagans do that?" (Matthew 5:43-47).

God calls us to be radically different than what we would expect. But how do we learn to truly love in the be-kind-to-your-enemies type of way? How do we love an ornery spouse? a pushy telemarketer? What does love in action look like?

Jesus gave us the perfect example. Throughout the Gospels we witness how Jesus treated people radically different than we do. I guarantee that a thoughtful, prayerful pass through the Gospels will grip you with the immense and overwhelming love of God. You won't walk away the same. John explains it to us in 1 John 4:7-12: "Dear friends, let us love one another, for love comes from God. Everyone who loves has been born of God and knows God. Whoever does not love does not know God, because God is love. This is how God showed his love among us: He sent his one and only Son into the world that we might live through him. This is love: not that we loved God, but that he loved us and sent his Son as an atoning sacrifice for our sins. Dear friends, since God so loved us, we also ought to love one another. No one has ever seen God; but if we love one another, God lives in us and his love is made complete in us."

That ornery spouse who sleeps next to you at night—God would have died just for him/her. That coworker who consistently steals your ideas—God would have died just for him. That roommate who never pulls her fair share of the weight—God would have died just for her. The person at church who's always talking behind your back—God would have died just for her. God calls us to be radically different. That's why He calls us the salt of the earth and the light of the world.

"You are the salt of the earth. But if the salt loses its saltiness, how can it be made salty again? It is no longer good for anything, except to be thrown out and trampled underfoot. You are the light of the world. A town built on a hill cannot be hidden. Neither do people light a lamp and put it under a bowl. Instead they put it on its stand, and it gives light to everyone in the house. In the same way, let your light shine before others, that they may see your good deeds and glorify your Father in heaven" (Matthew 5:13-16).

Here's some practical advice on enhancing your relationships: Let's not talk about it, let's *be* about it. Step out of your comfort zone. Do an experiment:

- If you're not naturally talkative, talk to five random people today. You will see people are more open than you think.
- If you're naturally talkative, *listen* to five random people today. You will see people have more to say than you think.
- Do something for someone before asking for something from him or her.
- In the middle of your next argument, remember that had salvation been only for the person in front of you, Jesus would have died just for him or her. It's an amazing combatant to anger. I've tried it before!

Mergers and Acquisitions

I've been blessed by the fact that my mother doesn't nag me into getting married. I believe it's because she realizes the art and science of a successful merger. In selecting a life partner, I've taken a three-pronged approach. I have opened myself to meeting someone who aligns with me logically, emotionally, and spiritually. But before you rush to write down such a calculated plan, let me give my disclaimer: I am grateful that God is a matchmaker, because otherwise, with this approach, I'd have to start requiring an application to find the perfect candidate. In talking with friends in similar situations, sometimes I think we have God working overtime in this area. I received my proof at the prayer seminar I mentioned in chapter 4; the facilitator shared that the most frequently occurring prayer request he receives is from people praying for a spouse. Wow! I would have never imagined in all his travels around the world that this would be so. In my mind this comment conjured up an image of a switchboard in heaven (think circa 1940s) with a circus of flashing lights and a tangle of cables. Every line ringing and buzzing at the same time with people requesting to be connected with so-and-so from English Lit 201 or such-and-such who sits in the third pew from the front at church. How does God keep it all straight? How can He provide for this unique need that humans have?

I found my answer in the last chapter of Esmie Branner's book *Beyond the Veil of Darkness*, in which she describes her experience in marrying a nominal Muslim man during a time when she was a nominal Christian. While I've read the book through several times, I've read the last chapter—in which she prays to God for her future husband—at least 20 times more.

After taking this journey with her over the course of the book, I've found that she is clearly a woman of faith. It's apparent that she is sincerely focused on relationship building with God. So after rebuilding her relationship with Him and seeking out His will, she determines that it is His will that she remarry. By this time Branner is so in love with Jesus that she wants to be in a relationship with someone with whom she can share that experience. So she begins to earnestly seek God, specifically asking for a husband.

After witnessing her experience with God, I determined that this was a Christian woman whose model I could follow, so I have taken to doing the same. I too am praying for my future husband. Now, this is not to say that I am singularly focused on getting married. In fact, I have been accused of the opposite. I was once told by a friend that I am not "committed to the project" (of getting married). She's probably right. While I feel as though I'm now ready to be married, I don't define myself by my singleness. It is my present state of being, but it is not who I am. I hope I am just as useful married as I am single. Granted, I'll spend more time ministering to my family, but it will still be a ministry. And at this moment in my life I have this weird sensation that God has an order to things. I don't have specific confirmation for this, but I do know that in Isaiah 55:8 God says, "For my thoughts are not your thoughts, neither are your ways my ways." And I know this is true, as I have seen door after door close in my life, allowing me to focus on where God wants me to be in *this* moment. I have applied for jobs that would have required my intense focus, and I have not received them. I have placed offers on a home, and they were not accepted. I have applied for graduate school, only to be waitlisted and then rejected. I have attempted to enter serious relationships, only to find something I couldn't get past. The only green light I have received, at *this* moment in my life, was to write *this* book. And as far as my eye can see, that's the piece of the journey God is showing me right now. In this process God has truly taught me the meaning of seeking first His kingdom and righteousness. He has shown me that when I do this, He will fulfill His part of the bargain, which is "all these things will be given to you" (Matthew 7:33).

So at the adequate time I will employ my three-pronged approach of aligning myself with someone logically, emotionally, and spiritually. In the meantime, here is what I have been learning. In graduate school I took a class called Finance and Accounting for Mergers and Acquisitions. After I crunched the numbers, what stuck out to me the most was that the human factor largely contributes to the success or failure of any merger or acquisition. A merger is thought of more as the combination of equals, so for our purposes we'll stick to that term. The purpose of a merger is to bring together two firms in order to create synergy, which basically means the two are stronger together than they were apart. They each bring something complementary to the table, thereby adding value to the other, as well as the ability to create something neither could have created alone. The value could be cost savings, increased revenue, or increased efficiency. Is that the point of marriage? Is your spouse a glorified roommate? Is he an extra income? If that were sufficient to make the marriage work, my guess is we would see a much higher success rate. But while those are *benefits* of the merger, they are not the merger's purpose.

The purpose of a merger is to create something with greater reach than either of the two individual entities had alone. For instance, if you sing and your spouse plays the piano, you are able to increase your reach by offering the world a duet instead of a solo. This is the logical aspect of the three-pronged approach. Will you create synergy with your spouse? Will the two of you have more reach than each of you would have had individually? Do you complement the other person's weaknesses? That is the first requirement in the merger.

We often place the majority of our focus on the emotional area of the merger, and when I was younger I was quite guilty of this. I dated for fun, for the thrill of it. But then I realized if I kept it up, I wouldn't have any of my heart left to give away to the man I planned to marry someday. Attraction is important, but never use this as the only factor in making a decision as important as marriage. Many a marriage has ended because what the couple thought was love didn't last. But I don't say this to understate the importance of attraction! Attraction is the flower on the fruit tree. All fruit trees flower before bearing fruit, but it's not the flowers that we eat. It's all about the fruit. And this brings me to the most important part of my approach: the spiritual aspect.

When deciding to align yourself with someone you must ask, *Will this person bring me closer to Christ?* This is the most important question of all. A trusted advisor once told me that when looking to enter a relationship with someone, I should always make sure that we are spiritually growing in the same direction. And this is very true. Will the merger bring you closer to God, or could it pull you away? Don't just answer this question from your current perspective. Do some examination, and please don't dismiss this by saying, "I will bring this person closer to God." Answer it from *their* perspective as well. Regardless of your goals, will the person bring *you* closer to God as well?

God is a God of relationships. I challenge you to mend any broken relationship you have in your life today. By doing so, you will be showing those around you an accurate picture of God. I challenge you to let Him direct your interactions with others, and I challenge you to trust Him with your romantic life. He will create a merger that will stand the test of time. As you begin to trust God with your relationships, He will be able to trust you with sharing an accurate picture of who He is with those around you.

Witnessing

Sharing Our Faith:
The Story of Paul and Silas

I had just sat down on one of the hard metal chairs in the waiting room when two blind men shuffled in from the opposite entrance, preceded by a helpful do-gooder. The rhythmic clack of their guide sticks served as a sound track. When the men finally took their seats, the do-gooder seemed to breathe a sigh of relief as he passed on his last bit of instructions. My year of studying Spanish in Spain allowed me to understand that the do-gooder was reaching into the recesses of his mind to dust off old Spanish phrases he hadn't used since second period high school Spanish class. At last he departed to catch his train. I sat back and released a small sigh, my own reward for a hard day's work. Just as my mind started to wander off, my thoughts were interrupted by a voice that was a little bit louder than the "inside voices" children are taught to use at a young age. In fact, the voice was obviously raised in an effort to attract attention. I pulled myself out of my thoughts.

"Hay alguien aqui quien hable español?" (Is there anyone here who speaks Spanish?) A few seconds passed, followed by silence. I kept to myself with my head buried in a book, in accordance with big city protocol. Again the question was asked, this time laced with a bit of disbelief. I joined the man in disbelief. In the heart of Chicago, surely someone in the room spoke Spanish. The blind man turned to his companion, muttering that he couldn't believe there wasn't anyone in the room who spoke Spanish. As if to allow someone who heard him the first time another opportunity, he asked the question again. This time I looked around the room to see if

there were any takers. No one. Slowly and reluctantly I turned toward the pair and asked, in Spanish, if the men needed help with anything. In that moment I learned my first lesson about witnessing. We each have a task to do—and when it's your turn, no one else can speak for you.

Guess what the man asked me. When I heard it, it left me surprised. He asked for the closest McDonald's. Contrary to popular belief, witnessing is not always about opening a Bible study and going through the texts. It's less about who you are when you're onstage and more about who you are when you're offstage. It's seldom about going door to door and often about opening your door to the opportunities and the possibilities you have to share a picture of the character of Christ with others.

It turns out that my blind Spanish inquisitor was hungry. And he wasn't asking me to buy him a meal. He simply wanted me to lead him to the nearest McDonald's. As I quickly turned the request over in my mind, I thought of the train that I would need to board shortly. Then I thought about the amount of time it would take me to guide him downstairs and return him back to the waiting room. I quickly came up with what I deemed to be a fair compromise. I offered to take the crumpled bill he held in his hand, run down to McDonald's, and return with his order: three hamburgers, hold everything but the lettuce.

While I thought this was the perfect solution, a look of skepticism quickly flashed across his face. Although I understood the reason for his mistrust, I didn't have time to convince him I wasn't out to get him. In his mind, I was just the random Spanish-speaking person in the room whom he couldn't see. So I thought of something I could say to infuse some trust, hoping to convince him of my good intentions: "I'm a Christian." As further proof of his skepticism, he immediately shot back, like a knee-jerk reflex, "If so, then give me the number of your pastor."

This made me think. Why aren't people more attracted to Christianity? Why doesn't the mere mention of Christ put those around us at ease? Why doesn't that one word conjure up a picture of trustworthiness? After mulling it over, I came to the conclusion that it's not because the love of Christ Himself is not compelling; it's because our demonstration of Christ's love is not compelling. For God is love, and He says, "I have loved you with an everlasting love; I have drawn you with unfailing kindness" (Jeremiah 31:3).

To ease his doubt, I gave in. As I led my blind Spanish-speaking companion out of the waiting room and toward the escalator, people glanced at us with curiosity. We walked almost side by side, his hand gently resting in the crook of my arm. Some gave approving nods, as they had previously stood by silently as the man shuffled along with his walking stick, asking anyone within the sound of his voice for help. We struggled through the revolving doors and then approached the escalator. No big deal if you can see, but a potential hazard if you're blind. I had taken these stairs numerous times and didn't think twice about them. I placed one foot on the first stair and he followed my lead. Then at the last minute, it occurred to me—we were on a set of rotating stairs. As the stairs moved, my blind Spanish-speaking companion seemed to lose his balance. In his attempt to steady himself, he grabbed my hand. My body stiffened at this practical yet seemingly intimate act. It's not often in Western society that we hold hands with one another. We expect it between lovers, children, and parents. But it's most uncomfortable in our society to hold the hand of a stranger; however, it was then I learned that, in sharing the love of Christ, we must do just that.

Couch Potato Christianity

I have a cold, hard truth to share with you: True Christianity can be quite uncomfortable. Truly reflecting the love of Christ disallows couch potato Christianity for two main reasons. As we show God to others, God pulls out a mirror and gives us a glimpse of ourselves. This is because as a sharer, it's easy to take on an "us" and "them" mentality. We will share our Jesus with you. As though we have everything to teach and nothing to learn. The reality is that when we share Christ with others, simultaneously God is trying to share Himself with us. We still need Jesus as much as those with whom we are sharing Him. Sometimes He gives us a reality check when our Christianity becomes a show. Thus, at times sharing Christ can be sobering, because often it is also when God shows us the areas in our lives that still require work. The best part is that this reality check provides us with the ideal attitude for sharing.

Another reason Christianity can be uncomfortable is that it asks us to do things that are unnatural to us. For instance, I believe we think God was talking to someone else when He said love your neighbor as yourself (Matthew 22:36-40), because this part of Christianity is uncomfortable. I've observed many Christians that are more passionate with a particular political view than they are with their love. According to Jesus, the most telling characteristic that is to be worn ostentatiously like a scarlet A on our chests is our love (John 13:34, 35). We are to care for the widows and the orphans (James 1:27). This is the true spirit of witnessing, loving one another as Jesus loves us.

And this is where all witnessing must begin—with Jesus. You can't sell something you're not willing to buy. If you're not already compelled by who God is, I would encourage you to read the Gospels. In fact, I would recommend getting the Bible on CD and listening to it while following along in your Bible (listening to *The Bible Experience* and reading along revolutionized my own spiritual life). The characters really come alive as you use multiple senses to go through Scripture. And when you further understand who Jesus is, you won't perceive the need to share Him as a *requirement* of your Christian curriculum. The reality is, you won't be able to keep silent about Him. "For Christ's love compels us, because we are convinced that one died for all, and therefore all died" (2 Corinthians 5:14). If you don't know where to start, here are some stories I'd recommend:

- Crucifixion and Resurrection (Matthew 27; 28)
- Invitation to the children (Matthew 19:13-15)
- Jesus calming the storm (Luke 8:22-25)
- Jesus' teaching on prayer (Luke 11:1-13)

These passages are just a few that have had an impact on my life. Continue to explore and seek God, and you will find Him, as we discussed in chapter 4, on prayer. The more clearly we know what the character of Christ looks like, the more honestly we can ask ourselves, "When people see us, whom will they see?" When the answer is Christ, then we are witnessing. It's a type of ambassadorship—a representation not of ourselves, but of God. We don't often think of it this way, but when people see us, we may be their only glimpse of God. Are we giving them an accurate depiction?

I thought about this while on an airplane one day. I broke airline travel protocol and started talking to the passenger on my right. After we exchanged a few questions, I discovered he was enlisted in the Air Force. He had been notified the day before that he was to fly to Maryland to teach a class. Perhaps in an act of defiance for the last-minute notice, he wore his civilian clothes. Had we not spoken, I would have mistaken him for a college kid with his trendy printed T-shirt, worn jeans, baseball cap, and wide leather bracelet. He mentioned that because he was on assignment he was supposed to be wearing his uniform, but he had opted not to. Is this how it can be with God? Can we take off our uniforms? Can we pick and choose when we want to represent God?

I must admit that at times I have taken off the uniform. The only problem is that people already know whom you claim to represent. For instance, whether I have a good day or a bad day at work, I still claim to represent God. The thought of that gives me a knot in my stomach as I think of the numerous times I've misrepresented God. If I were representing myself, it would be OK for people to know that at times I feel like being there and at other times I don't. But Colossians 3:23, 24 tells us, "Whatever you do, work at it with all your heart, as working for the Lord, not for human masters, since you know that you will receive an inheritance from the Lord as a reward. It is the Lord Christ you are serving." So when I think about the fact that I may be the only picture of God a person might ever see, it's quite sobering. In order to stand up to this challenge we must be in constant communion with God. Contrary to Christian legend, we weren't called to win others over by using only our religion.

Too often we're encouraged to share our religion with others and not necessarily our relationship with God. Perhaps it's because we can hide behind a set of beliefs without exposing too much of ourselves. We can try to win them over without being vulnerable and honest about the Christian struggle. But 2 Corinthians 12:9, 10 says, "'My grace is sufficient for you, for my power is made perfect in weakness.' Therefore I will boast all the more gladly about my weaknesses, so that Christ's power may rest on me. That is why, for Christ's sake, I delight in weaknesses, in insults, in hardships, in persecutions, in difficulties. For when I am weak, then I am strong." This verse is the gas that powers the engine of the Christian experience: knowing that despite who we are, God is able to create something amazing. That's the essence of the good news—we are receiving something we don't deserve. Witnessing is about showing people a picture of Christ, and what better picture of Him than the one exhibited in our relationship with Him, showing that He loves us in spite of our weaknesses.

I must admit that sometimes the idea of witnessing can seem a bit intimidating, as though we're imposing our beliefs on someone else. Witnessing, proselytizing, sharing the faith—no matter how you slice it, the concept often gets a bad rap. I have often been fearful in my own life to take the steps necessary to witness. I have balked at talking about my beliefs and have squirmed at the thought of inviting someone to church. But a recent experience with a friend has helped me put this idea into perspective.

While I was chatting over the Internet with a friend, he told me he might be suffering from an incurable disease. He wouldn't receive the results until the following week. I attempted to say calming things. I told him that God is in control and that he could rest in that. While the phrases that popped out of my mouth most likely oozed with the expected sappiness of Christian clichés, I sincerely believed in what I was saying. I felt as though I was getting through to him and providing him comfort—until his words broke through my rhetoric.

"I

AM

AFRAID!"

In that brief exchange we shared a rare moment of vulnerability. It's not often in the human experience people share their fears with one another. But if words were allowed to be free, we would see an alarming amount of honesty. Those three words speak volumes into the human experience, because at the crux of the human experience is fear. We fear missing out, growing old, being alone, or being broke or sick. We fear death. And I'm sure you could add a few additional items to the list of your biggest fears.

Whether you believe in God or not, the presence of evil in our world is quite evident. On this point there is no philosophical debate. The incurable disease of sin is the reason for the evil we experience in our world. Our friends and family members are also suffering from this incurable disease, and we attempt to give them calming words on how they can deal with their situations. But their silent cries break through our attempts:

I

AM

AFRAID!

The good news is there is a solution for fear. In 2 Timothy 1:7, 8 Paul shares that "for the Spirit God gave us does not make us timid, but gives us power, love and self-discipline. So do not be ashamed of the testimony about our Lord." Perhaps with this confidence and urgency, Paul and Silas (and numerous others throughout the course of history) were able to undergo dangerous situations to share Jesus.

In Acts 16:16-34 we find Paul and Silas in the middle of missionary work. As they were headed toward the river, where the Jews in the area held their worship service, a local demon-possessed slave girl, who was known to be a fortuneteller, followed them around, shouting, "These men are servants of the Most High God, who are telling you the way to be saved" (verse 17). Although the message was true, the messenger was quite distracting. "Finally Paul became so annoyed that he turned around and said to the spirit, 'In the name of Jesus Christ I command you to come out of her!' At that moment the spirit left her" (verse 18).

While I imagine that the slave girl was happy to be freed of the spirit, her owners did not share her sentiments. As far as they were concerned, Paul and Silas were messing with their money. They immediately had them arrested and dragged into the public courtyard.

The slave owners carefully crafted their argument to push the buttons of the Roman authorities. Somehow the "casting out demons" story didn't seem like it would hold up in court. "These men are Jews, and are throwing our city into an uproar by advocating customs unlawful for us Romans to accept or practice" (verses 20, 21), they claimed. That did the trick. Paul and Silas were publicly beaten and imprisoned. At this point in the story most of us would have begun to question God and His intentions. Surely Paul and Silas were being obedient to God by worshipping with fellow believers and casting out demons. After such faithfulness, why would God allow them to end up in such a predicament? What was God's purpose in this situation?

I often like to imagine that God has His people like chess pieces on a chessboard. The unskilled eye is unaware and baffled by the way the chess master moves His pieces. This is because the common observer sees only the present move; however, the chess master is always thinking several steps ahead. If God were not thinking ahead in this situation, why else would He have placed Paul and Silas in jail for an overnight stay?

As we pause from the story, think through your life. Where has God place you that at first appearance was unseemly and inconvenient? Were the accommodations not what you expected and the people not as friendly as they should have been? Throughout the world, God knows that He has people who are in need of Him, who are suffering from an incurable disease without knowing it. There are people who want to know more about Him and His love. In order to reach them, He oftentimes moves the pieces on the board to make His move to connect those in need with those who are best able to reach them. We must make ourselves available for these opportunities.

A Hollywood writer couldn't have crafted this story better. All during their time in the jail cell Paul and Silas continued to praise God and sing songs that expressed their faith and joy in God. Suddenly, around midnight, there was an earthquake that loosened their hand and feet cuffs. The jailer immediately woke up and saw that the jail doors were open. He probably screamed. A jailer who loses his prisoners is like a doctor who kills his patients. At that moment he must have thought he had nothing to live for, so he took his sword and prepared to end it all, thus avoiding a beheading because of the mishap he thought had happened under his watch.

When Paul noticed this, he called out, "Don't hurt yourself; we're all still here."

I'm sure a mix of emotions washed over the jailer: relief, confusion, joy, embarrassment. At that moment the jailer, who earlier had ridiculed Paul and Silas, was now open to hear what they had to say. Paul took this opportunity to share Jesus with him and his family, and the jailer was so moved by what he saw and heard that he asked Paul to baptize him then and there.

Types of Witnessing

Acting on What You Know

The word *witnessing* immediately conjures up (for me, at least) images of choir attire, black pants and a white shirt, walking around the neighborhood with a book in hand. Now contrast that image with this: You're on *The Apprentice* (Donald Trump's show that approaches business like a grade school game of dodge ball), and your team has been given the task of getting the word out about a new miracle product. All the research shows that this product is lifesaving, but few people know about it, and most who are aware of it have not tried it for themselves. Enter Team Born to Win (insert yourself on that team). You must come up with the most effective strategy to market the chosen product. How would you approach this task? Now take this concept and think of the best way you can reach your peers, coworkers, and neighbors. Think of how you can share the love of Christ with them. Often it may not be that they are unreceptive to hearing the good news, but unlike Paul and Silas, we don't present a pretty picture that allows our listeners to be very open to what we have to say.

While the success of sharing God with others is dependent upon the Holy Spirit and not us and our abilities, we can still wrap the good news in the pretty wrapping paper it deserves.

Perhaps more effective than verbally sharing Jesus is for others to see you doing actions that reflect Jesus. For instance, if we are His representatives, can we simply walk past those who are suffering? How can we pull ourselves out of our comfort zone and really reflect the love of Christ? Here are some suggestions:

- Give the homeless money or food. And don't just give it to them—acknowledge them. We often say we don't understand how other cultures have "untouchables," but in many ways we have the same concept built into our society. Acknowledge everyone around you.
- Speak to the cleaning people in your building.
- Visit those in nursing homes.
- Send an anonymous gift to someone in hospice care.
- Send a card to a friend you haven't seen in a while.
- Spend time with a young person who might look up to you.
- Call a widow long after others have stopped grieving with her.
- Celebrate good news with a friend.
- Reach out to an enemy.

Sharing What/Whom You Know

It wasn't until Paul and Silas gave an unexpected glimpse of the character of Christ that the jailer wanted to know more. As cliché as it sounds, seeing really is believing. We often skip this first type of witnessing of acting on what we know and move on to the second type, which is sharing what we know. Of course it's much easier to tell than it is to show, but often people don't want to hear what you have to say until they see what you are doing. Think of it as building credibility.

Have you ever found a deal that was so good you had to pass the information on to your friends and family, perhaps a special on gas, clothes, or food that was just too good to keep to yourself? As a Christian, do you feel the same way about the love of Christ? Is it so great that you feel you must share it with those around you? This type of witnessing should be the typical kind we think of—sharing our relationship with God with others and inviting them to experience the same thing.

Clarifying Information

Sometimes we are called to clarify someone's understanding of something. The person may already be in the perfect place for relationship building, and we are called solely to explain a point. In Acts 8:26-40 we see Philip being asked by God to meet the Ethiopian eunuch and explain to him the scriptures found in Isaiah. The eunuch makes a powerful statement in response to Philip's inquiring if he understands what he is reading. He responds, "How can I, unless someone explains it to me?"

Surprisingly, my blind Spanish inquisitor was not the only visually impaired person I had in my life at that time. I also had a friend who was struggling to see a clear picture of God. And to be honest with you, I was struggling to show him a clear picture as well. I needed to heed Peter's urging to "always be prepared to give an answer to everyone who asks you to give a reason for the hope that you have" (1 Peter 3:15).

We often danced around the conversation, always careful not to step on one another's toes, but we never delved deeply. At the time I had a very "live and let live" attitude, and I thought it was inappropriate to impose my beliefs on him. I figured if he had questions, he would ask. To be honest, however, part of me was always afraid of being rejected.

While he had grown up in a faith community, he didn't own a Bible at the time of our meeting, and he had a lot of internal questions about God. Looking back, I see that I had opportunity after opportunity to share a picture of Jesus with Him. And though I did in my actions, I was never able "to give a reason for the hope I have." Since then, the opportunity has seemed to elude me. While verbally he agreed to let me share a picture of Jesus with him, he always seems to be busy, and the actual moment seemed as though it would never arrive.

As I continuously brought this concern before God, one morning as I opened my Bible to the Gospels to do some research for this book, the Bible providentially opened to the most telling chapter that gave me assurance that God will make the blind in my life see. It was the story of Jesus healing a man born blind, found in John 9.

Jesus always took advantage of teachable moments with His disciples; sometimes He found the lesson in nature, and other times He found the lesson in human nature. On this particular day, as He was walking along with His disciples, He spotted a blind man begging by the side of the road. While seeing those with physical disabilities was common, this time the disciples were impressed to ask:

"'Rabbi, who sinned, this man or his parents, that he was born blind?' 'Neither this man nor his parents sinned,' said Jesus, 'but this happened so that the works of God might be displayed in him'" (John 9:2, 3).

This was the first aha! moment for me. While this verse is talking of physical blindness, I was assured that the spiritually blind man in my life would also be presented an opportunity from God for His character to be revealed in his life.

Now back to the man in John 9. He was probably so unsuspecting that day. He woke up and patted his way around his little room and gathered his clay begging pot. He counted the steps to the door and grabbed his seeing-eye stick right next to the post. One, two, three, four, five ... OK, right turn. He knew it was 24 steps to the spot he staked out every day. All he needed was a little bit to help him make it through the day. That was his primary objective: survival. To him, that was pretty much all there was.

Because he could not see, he relied a lot on his other senses. As he manned his begging station he listened to footsteps and snippets of conversations. He probably heard sounds of a group of small children, taking him back to his childhood. There was a cart going by; perhaps a vendor. Now he heard a large group approaching, and then they stopped directly in front of him. It sounded as if one Man spoke above the rest. His mind tried to penetrate the conversation. *They're talking about me,* he likely thought to himself.

Then the most unusual thing happened. The Man who spoke to the rest stopped speaking. He then heard the sound of spitting. The blind man heard some rustling, and then he felt a warm, gooey substance placed on his eyes. Had this been any other scenario, with any other group of people, he would have been upset—but something about the Man's voice gave him a gentle reassurance. "Go, wash in the Pool of Siloam" (John 9:7).

So the blind man picked himself up with the help of his seeing-eye stick and began to make his way to the pool—36 steps from his station. When the man arrived at the pool, he knew it because of the sounds of the water lapping at the edges. He heard the sounds of children. There was a sense of levity at the pool. The man lowered himself next to the water. Though he didn't know who this Man was, he felt compelled to do as He had told him to do. He cupped a bit of water in his hands and created a small puddle in his hands to rinse off his eyes. The water gently rinsed away the gooey substance and at the instant his eyes were clean the man exclaimed, "I can see!"

After settling in and getting used to this new vision, the man ran home and began to discover everything. He had painted a mental picture of what things looked like, but with his new vision he no longer had to imagine.

Upon seeing him, his neighbors and friends were floored. The conversation went back and forth; some thought it was him while others thought it was someone else. He stood there and tried to assure them that he was the former blind man. But they were so engrossed in their arguments that they didn't let Exhibit A speak for himself. So finally, to settle it, they decided to take the man to the Pharisees in the synagogue. Surely they would be able to settle this.

Though they pitched the idea to the man as a suggestion, the push of the crowd gave him little option in the matter. As further support, they brought the man's parents as well. But even his parents were amazed. Though they claimed him, they didn't want any part of this confusion, so they encouraged the Pharisees to question the man himself.

"He's an adult, he can speak for himself," they claimed.

"'Give glory to God by telling the truth,' [the Pharisees] said. 'We know this man [Jesus] is a sinner.' He [the man] replied, 'Whether he is a sinner or not, I don't know. One thing I do know. I was blind but now I see'" (verses 24, 25).

After our visit to McDonald's, I took my blind Spanish-speaking companion to church with me. The members loved him and were ecstatic to hear his testimony and listen to his music. After church I returned him downtown, where we had met. I was always a bit uncomfortable during our encounters or on the phone. I never knew exactly what to say or do, but I tried to help him the best I could. I never saw him again, but during the time he was in my life I tried to lend him my eyes. Now I am aware that I frequently run into the spiritually blind. And in the case with my friend, I have some assurance that he will spiritually see, because Jesus said in John 9, "For judgment I have come into this world, so that the blind will see and those who see will become blind" (verse 39). One day he will no longer have to accept other people's descriptions of reality. He will be able to perceive for himself.

Through all of this I was surprised to learn that when it comes to sharing my faith, I'm quite intimidated by risk. Perhaps it's because my God gauge is off. Perhaps I've misperceived who God really is.

Risking It All

Taking a Risk for God:
The Story of Esther /
The Workers and the Talents

've always imagined God as a Superman type of God, rescuing damsels in distress when they screech out a cry for help. I've imagined Him swooping the person out of the precarious situation and rushing them to a safe place. But as I look over the experiences in my life and the lives of many in the Bible, I'm beginning to realize that He's more of a MacGyver type of God.

My childhood is best understood through a love-hate relationship I had with my brother, who's five years older. While he was my shining star and could typically do no wrong in my eyes, there were moments I built up seething resentment toward him—when we watched TV. The primary problem was that he had all power over the remote control. The only moments I got to catch a snippet of one of my favorite shows were the times he got up to refill his Kool-Aid or get another bowl of cereal. Upon his return, the station was promptly returned to "his show," and MacGyver fell into that category.

I remember MacGyver as frequently being caught in a bind and, through his mechanical genius, always managing to disable a bomb or stop a world of other catastrophes from wreaking havoc. Somehow the outcome of his emergencies always seemed to hinge on his being able to complete the task under the most auspicious and barely believable constraints of time and physical obstacles.

As I've matured in my Christian walk, I'm beginning to see that though MacGyver is a very flawed example of God's working in our lives, he serves to illustrate the difference between two perspectives about God. In the perspective of the MacGyver God, instead of swooping us out of the grips of the problem, He will guide us *through* the problem, teaching us valuable skills and life lessons, and strengthening our faith along the way. Oftentimes we are unable to see the solution until we've taken the first step of faith. Too often in my Christian walk, my flawed understanding of this concept has caused me to lose faith and at times become angry with God for not moving as I expected. It's also for this reason that I've often failed to take risks for God.

In college I majored in finance. One of the major premises of the subject is the concept of risk and return. The amount of return you receive on an investment is directly related to the amount of risk you take. A quick review of Matthew 25:14-30 makes me wonder if God was teaching business concepts in His parable of the talents. My guess is that Jesus told the story, not in an effort to create a Wall Street mogul, but to teach an even further-reaching concept. Each worker was given some money to invest in Moneybag Mitchell's business. Though not explicitly stated, there must have been some element of risk in investing it.

Before we dive into this story, let's look at how risk relates to relationship building and restoration with God. Risk is the measure of possibility of things working or not working as you anticipate. Risk is involved in every aspect of our lives, and not being willing to take risks can negatively impact lives in many ways, including spiritually. Understanding how risk plays into the relationship-building process will allow us to apply concepts taught in the story of the talents.

A trusted counselor once told me to focus on those things I that *can* control. Adding that concept to faith in God is powerful insurance. Insurance is the guarantee that you will be able to handle the risk in your life, and there are many risks involved in a relationship with God. But we must know that we are covered. For example, there is a risk involved in committing to a relationship with God. You may wonder how your friends, family, and coworkers will react. Will they be supportive of your decision? Don't worry—you're covered. In Joshua 1:5 God says, "I will never leave you nor forsake you."

There is also risk involved in praying. God may or may not answer as you expect, but you're covered. You're guaranteed that God will hear you and answer as promised: "Then you will call on me and come and pray to me, and I will listen to you" (Jeremiah 29:12). And you're guaranteed that

His answer will be the best thing for you. "Every good and perfect gift is from above, coming down from the Father of the heavenly lights, who does not change like shifting shadows (James 1:17).

There is risk in deciding to be different from everyone else to celebrate the Sabbath. You may think it will interfere with your work schedule. No worries; you're covered. "And my God will meet all your needs according to the riches of his glory in Christ Jesus" (Philippians 4:19).

You will be taking a risk when you reach out in love to your enemies. What if it seems as if they've gotten the best of you? God has you covered. "The Lord will fight for you; you need only to be still" (Exodus 14:14). "Do not take revenge, my dear friends, but leave room for God's wrath, for it is written: 'It is mine to avenge; I will repay,' says the Lord" (Romans 12:19).

One of the biggest risks you take may be when you share God's love with others. You may feel very vulnerable in the process. You may feel at risk of being rejected. You have the biggest coverage of all on this risk: "So is my word that goes out from my mouth: It will not return to me empty, but will accomplish what I desire and achieve the purpose for which I sent it" (Isaiah 55:11).

Now that we see the connection between risk, relationship building, and restoration, let's dive in.

Talented

Moneybag Mitchell walked into his office and gave a long, sweeping glance over his desk. As he pulled out his well-tattered checklist he noticed that one thing was still left undone—and a very important thing at that. He quickly went outside and called for his workers. As he watched them approach the house he thought over the modest business he had started a few years back, after he'd finished his apprenticeship. At the time it was only him. He dealt with all aspects of the business, from sales to purchasing to maintaining relationship with his customers. These days he was fortunate enough to have a few extra hands to help bear the load.

Upon the workers' arrival, Moneybag Mitchell looked at each man with careful consideration. He felt confident about going on his trip to buy merchandise and leaving the three to hold down the fort. He reached deep into the pouch he kept tied around his waist and began to speak.

"As you know, I am preparing to head out to buy merchandise for the business. In my absence, Industrious Ivan, I've decided to give you a budget of $10,000. Loquacious Lou, you will receive a $4,000 budget. Cautious

Cal, you will receive a $2,000 budget. I'm expecting some solid ideas to help make the business grow."

Without much ado, Moneybag Mitchell handed out the money just as he had stated and then set out on his long journey. The next day the men scurried around like little worker bees; they sketched out ideas and sent envoys to do due diligence work. Each man had a group of advisors giving suggestions on where the funds would be best invested to make the biggest return. As the weeks went by, new vendor stands littered the road leading up to the property. Each business boasted more potential than the one before.

One day the three workers gathered for a business meeting over lunch. Because each man had been fairly absorbed in his projects, little had been discussed about the progress they were making in investing Moneybag Mitchell's money. Instead they casually discussed the weather and gave updates on the wife and kids, all the while carefully sidestepping the most obvious conversation of all.

Finally it was evident that Loquacious Lou, like an overfilled water balloon, was on the verge of bursting from his eagerness to update the others on his progress. He was a talker, so it was no surprise that he struggled to keep from sharing his progress. Because of his gift of gab, all of Lou's business ideas capitalized on sales, gauging the customers' needs and making them feel comfortable. However, he did express a few downfalls, and Cautious Cal winced in pain. Cal quickly quipped how Moneybag Mitchell would be very disappointed if Loquacious Lou ended up losing some of his money. Lou quickly replied that it was OK that he had experienced a few challenges, as he still planned to double Moneybag Mitchell's money. A look of skepticism settled on Cautious Cal's face.

Industrious Ivan then decided to share a few of the ideas he was pursuing. Because of his wide variety of talents, including his ability to flawlessly craft Moneybag Mitchell's products, as well as communicate and sell, each idea brimmed with promise. Overwhelmed with curiosity, Loquacious Lou ventured to ask, "Have they all worked out? Has every single idea gone according to plan?"

With a bit of hesitation, Industrious Ivan replied honestly that he had experienced a few setbacks. He did have a couple of obstacles to overcome, but he was moving forward. Cautious Cal remained as quiet as a mute.

As the three men finished lunch, Cautious Cal reached for the pouch he kept carefully hidden beneath his outer robes. He fingered the coins given to him by Moneybag Mitchell. Safe, sound, and intact, just as he had received them. He had always been one to be overly guarded, carefully weighing his options before a big decision, which in many situations had proven to be beneficial. In fact, he had often been complimented for this ability.

Soon after the meeting, when Cal's wife realized he had brought the pouch to bed, she drew the line and told him he had taken his caution and apprehension too far. It was evident that this gift had become a burden. In her frustration she urged him to deposit the money. Then at least he would earn some interest.

Cautious Cal gave the idea a quick once-over in his mind, then immediately dismissed it. What if the markets suddenly collapsed? Not on his watch! Moneybag Mitchell would get his money back just as it had been given, with the exact same coins in the exact same order.

One evening, under the guise of getting some vegetables from the garden, Cautious Cal got the clever idea to bury the coins. He amused himself at his own "wisdom." Why hadn't he thought of this earlier? While digging up some vegetables, Cautious Cal paused to dig a deep hole right next to the sycamore tree, so that he could remember where the money was hidden.

After what seemed like an eternity to his wife she called out to him, asking about the vegetables. At this he quickly brushed himself off, gathered his things, and hurried back toward the house. A sense of self-satisfaction settled over him. He wouldn't be like his foolhardy coworkers and put Moneybag Mitchell's money at risk. He'd make sure he could return the money just as it was received.

A great deal of time went by, longer than anyone had expected. The seasons changed several times over without word from Moneybag Mitchell. But each man carried on with his normal duties and with his life responsibilities.

One day during the lunch hour a lone rider approached Moneybag Mitchell's property. He announced Moneybag Mitchell's eminent return. The men scrambled to pull things together. Although the operation ran fairly smoothly in Moneybag Mitchell's absence, they wanted to make sure all was in order. Because Industrious Ivan and Loquacious Lou were so thoroughly engrossed in preparing their reports for Moneybag Mitchell, Cautious Cal quietly slipped out the back door, unnoticed, to run home as quickly as possible.

Cautious Cal's eyes scanned the garden until they fell upon the sycamore tree. He ran to the tree and immediately fell to the ground. His hands began digging ferociously, like a little puppy in frantic search of a hidden bone. When he did not find the pouch right away, a sinking feeling flooded over him. He made another attempt to locate it. Finally his hands struck the gold. He pulled the pouch from its hiding place and brushed himself off. Immediately he set off to return to Moneybag Mitchell's property.

Cautious Cal slipped in the back door of the house and casually walked into the room where the other two were gathered. Though he attempted to appear carefree, the careful observer could easily note his disheveled appearance and the agitation on his face. Because Industrious Ivan and Loquacious Lou paced back and forth, practicing their presentations for Moneybag Mitchell, they hardly took notice when Cautious Cal reentered the room.

Within a matter of minutes after Cautious Cal's arrival, a hacking noise broke the silence in the room. All three of the men stopped. Upon seeing its source, the three men quickly fell in line, like little tin soldiers in a window display.

Moneybag Mitchell's eyes were kind yet expectant. "How have things gone in my absence? Everything appears to be in order."

Although the moments prior to Moneybag Mitchell's arrival were filled with anticipation, now that it had finally arrived, Industrious Ivan and Loquacious Lou felt a sense of calm wash over them.

"I'd be glad to update you," volunteered Industrious Ivan. "When you left, you entrusted me with $10,000. I know you hired me for my salesmanship, as well as my ability to flawlessly create your products, so I expanded your business using those skills. I also used several of the methods you taught me."

As Industrious Ivan spoke, he periodically etched pictures and diagrams on a small tablet to illustrate some of the ideas he had implemented.

"So while you gave me $10,000, through the various ventures I've just described to you, I'm happy to return $20,000 to you."

Upon hearing this, Moneybag Mitchell beamed with joy. "Well done, good and faithful servant; you were faithful over a few things, I will make you ruler over many things. Enter into the joy of your Lord" (Matthew 25:21, NKJV).

With a look of expectancy, Moneybag Mitchell's eyes fell on Loquacious Lou. As if on cue, he stood and began his presentation. He showed Moneybag Mitchell the scrolls where he'd maintained records of his transactions. Additionally, he shared a sample of the product he happened to have on hand. Throughout the entire presentation Moneybag Mitchell seemed fully engaged. Lou concluded with the most interesting part of all, the return on his investment.

"Moneybag Mitchell, you gave me $4,000 when you left here. I am happy to return $8,000 to you."

Moneybag Mitchell, now overwhelmed with joy, gave Loquacious Lou a hearty pat on the back, along with a firm handshake. He looked him directly in the eyes with a look of satisfaction.

After the strong performances from Industrious Ivan and Loquacious Lou, Moneybag Mitchell waited in great anticipation for Cautious Cal's report. He had a sense of confidence, as he had already seen how each man's talents and abilities were matched by his returns. When he hired Cautious Cal, he recognized his enormous potential and careful ways, and he expected a positive report from him as well.

At this time all eyes landed on Cautious Cal. He fumbled nervously with the pouch tucked beneath his robe. His skeptical predictions of failure for Industrious Ivan and Loquacious Lou had proved not to be true. When he did not immediately speak up, he received a look from Moneybag Mitchell that gave him a prod.

"Uhm . . ."

He cleared his throat, partially out of necessity but mostly in an attempt to ensure his voice was still working.

"Speak up," Moneybag Mitchell urged.

"Well, sir, I mean, 'Lord, I knew you to be a hard man, reaping where you have not sown, and gathering where you have not scattered seed. And I was afraid, and went and hid your [money] in the ground. Look, there you have what is yours'" (verses 24, 25, NKJV).

Moneybag Mitchell's face glazed over as he said, "You wicked and lazy servant, you knew that I reap where I have not sown and gather where I have not scattered seed. So you ought to have deposited my money with the bankers, and at my coming I would have received back my own with interest" (verses 26, 27, NKJV).

Moneybag Mitchell proceeded to command Cautious Cal to instead turn over the $2,000 to Ivan, who had been entrusted with $10,000 and doubled it.

"For to everyone who has, more will be given, and he will have abundance; but from him who does not have, even what he has will be taken away" (verse 29, NKJV).

Prior to writing this chapter, I never really identified with Cautious

Cal's experience. I always told myself that I am using my abilities to further God's kingdom. But when I put the story in perspective and realized that it shows Cautious Cal's unwillingness to take a risk for Moneybag Mitchell's business, something rang very true for me. I almost wanted to join "Non-Risk-Takers for Jesus Anonymous."

But as I mentioned earlier, my unwillingness to take a risk was based on my perspective of God. When I had the Superman perspective of God, I believed the answers to my prayers would magically appear without my participation. I wouldn't have to talk, walk, or interact with anyone in order to see the answer. I would not experience discomfort, embarrassment, or unease, and *never* would I *ever* have to take any risks, because my "Superman" God would never ask me to do anything uncomfortable. He would always deliver the solution to the problem to my front door.

Don't get me wrong: Jesus *is* my all in all. However, it doesn't mean that He wouldn't have me take an active role in my own life. In fact, there are many examples in the Bible in which we are able to see God's working *because* the people involved were willing to step out in faith and do what God commanded. Consider Naaman (2 Kings 5:1-14), Noah (Genesis 6), Hosea (Hosea 1), Abraham (Genesis 22:1-19), just to name a few. And if you want to see the Hall of Fame of biblical risk takers, visit Hebrew 11, which is often referred to as the faith chapter. This gives us a rundown of people through the ages who not only claimed faith, but also had the courage to exercise that faith. And this is what God expects from us, because "without faith it is impossible to please God" (Hebrews 11:6). He might actually want to use you in many more ways than you're allowing Him, and He may be able to do this only after you permit Him to change your perspective.

I'm not sure of the exact way Esther's perspective of God changed after she saw how He worked in such an amazing way in her life, but I do know that she had an enormous amount of faith, which allowed her the courage to take a huge risk for God. The first part of her story has all the makings of a romance (minus the part when the King "tried out" his potential wives before actually choosing one). The beautiful, small town orphan girl becomes royalty—a feel-good story fit for the Hallmark channel.

However, as you read the book of Esther, you quickly notice that this frilly love story very soon becomes a suspenseful story filled with treachery and deceit, which was often fueled by the characters' oversized egos. Here's the Cliffs Notes-like version to get you up to speed.

Characters You Need to Know

Esther—young Jewish girl with the unlikely story of becoming queen. Raised by Mordecai, her cousin.

Vashti—king's first wife, who was banished from the kingdom because of her disobedience to the king.

King Ahasuerus—king of Medes and Persians. Ruled 127 provinces, from India to Ethiopia.

Mordecai—raised his cousin Esther. Saved King Ahasuerus from an assassination attempt.

Haman—in charge of all princes. Hated Mordecai because he would not bow down in front of him. Attempted to kill all of the Jews as a result.

Hegai—king's eunuch, custodian of king's harem.

Setting

Shusan, the citadel, modern-day Susa of Iran

The story of Esther is almost like a biblical Cinderella story, perhaps with the title "Hidden Identity: From Orphan Girl to Queen of Medes and Persians." Among all the women in the kingdom, the king chose Esther as his wife.

The king had just thrown a larger-than-life party that lasted 180 days. And as if that weren't enough, he decided to throw a weeklong after party. Cycling through the ways the king decided to entertain himself, he thought of one last thing he had not yet done: show off his most precious possessions. I can only imagine the people oohing and aahing over the king's jewels, clothes, servants, and homes. As the king basked in the attention he thought to himself, *Let me show off my most precious possession of all: my wife, Queen Vashti.*

The king's eunuch brought the request to Vashti, and upon hearing it, Vashti both agreed and disagreed. On one hand, Vashti had no doubt of her worth to the king. On the other hand, she felt she was *so* precious that she shouldn't be shown off at a party like a common plaything. And while we're not given insight into this in the Bible, I can only imagine that this wasn't the first time Vashti expressed her opinion (perhaps with some attitude) to her husband. The problem was that *this* time she had done it in front of all of "his boys," which was totally unacceptable for the king. After all, if the king couldn't get his wife to listen to him, how would he get others to listen? At the advice of his wise men ("his boys") the king banished Vashti from the palace in an effort to keep the other women in the kingdom in line.

After the party ended and "his boys" were gone, it didn't take long for the king to realize that he had just made a very serious decision. His wife was gone, and although he had sent her away it didn't lessen the sting of the decision, so he began to sulk. After witnessing the effects of this decision on the king, one of his officials suggested he put out a call to all of the young virgins in the land in search of a new queen. Consider it an ancient form of Match.com.

So the officials gathered the eligible young women from around the kingdom for the king to begin his search. Politely speaking, as the king sought out his perfect match, he "visited" with each of the women and then sent them to his harem the next morning. This went on for quite some time, but none of the women seemed to catch his fancy.

Finally, many beauty treatments later, it was Esther's turn. All the eunuchs and servants were rooting for Esther. There was something about her. I'm not sure if she made them feel comfortable in her presence, if she won them over with her smile, or if she looked them in the eye when she spoke and made them feel like the only person in the room. But with her grace, she managed to win over all of the palace staff she encountered, and all the servants (especially Hegai, the king's eunuch) were hoping that when Esther had her turn with the king, he would see what they saw. Sure enough, after the king spent time with Esther, he was lovestruck. There truly was something about Esther (she was obviously a Proverbs 31 woman).

So the king had a new wife and Esther a new home. And while things were happy on the home front, trouble was brewing outside of the palace gates. There was a man, Haman, with a rather large ego who worked for the king. In fact, not only did he work for the king—he was in charge of all of the princes. Because of his position in the kingdom there was a rule that whenever he came around, everyone in his presence had to bow down. While some people may have had problems with it, they sucked it up and concluded that this was the way things were and that they were not going to change. That is, everyone except for Mordecai.

Whenever Haman came around, he could be sure to find a sea of heads bowed in deference to him. The first time Haman noticed Mordecai, he perhaps thought it was a mistake. However, upon second glance, the defiance that Mordecai's unbowed head symbolized caused Haman to consider this a deliberate act of insolence, and he determined that he would not be made to look like a fool. Haman then plotted to get rid of Mordecai, and all the people like him—the Jews.

Imagine that. A man gets mad at you and then plots to kill everyone like you. All blonds. All book lovers. All lefties. All people from Seattle. Wiped off the earth. All because of one man's grudge.

When Mordecai heard this, he was distraught—so much so that he started wailing hysterically. He tore his clothes in anguish and covered himself with ashes. It must have been an overwhelming sight to see.

Soon after, Mordecai sent Esther a very sobering message:

"Do not think in your heart that you will escape in the king's palace any more than all the other Jews. For if you remain completely silent at this time, relief and deliverance will arise for the Jews from another place, but you and your father's house will perish. Yet who knows whether you have come to the kingdom for such a time as this?" (Esther 4:13, 14, NKJV).

At the time of Mordecai's request Esther had not told the king that she was Jewish. But suddenly her identity became very important.

This was one of my favorite stories as a kid because it has the themes all young girls love: royalty, beauty, and the triumph of an orphan girl. But what has always stood out to me is the line "Who knows whether you have come to the kingdom for such a time as this?" What a powerful suggestion that speaks volumes into the story! While the problem has not yet been solved, it is now clear to Esther that she could be a part of a divine appointment. The question is how she will respond.

Before we reveal *what* Esther did, let's look at *how* she got there. After facing her problem, Esther took the following steps:

Esther called for a time of fasting and praying. When Esther learned of the law that had just been issued, she told Mordecai to get the Jews together and to have them fast and pray for three days. She said that she and her servants would do the same. While Esther knew that something must be done, she decided to consult with God before making a move. She wanted to make sure that she showed God her dependence upon Him and that she placed herself in a position to hear Him when He spoke to her.

Esther took the decision she had made to the Lord. Esther assessed the situation and saw that Mordecai was asking her to speak with the king to intervene on behalf of the Jews. Both Mordecai and Esther had MacGyver views of God. They believed God had placed Esther in this situation in order to appeal to the king as his wife. They did not believe that it was their role simply to sit back and watch. Instead, they believed they were called to take an active role in receiving their answer to prayer.

Esther acted upon her decision. Once the designated time of fasting had passed, Esther moved forward and acted upon her risky decision.

Now that we have looked at the steps Esther took, let's get back to the action. In the end it was obvious to Esther that the only option she had was to plead with the king on behalf of her people. Despite her beauty and grace, and despite being the queen, even Esther had boundaries in the king's house. Approaching the king without being invited would almost guarantee sudden punishment. And after his dealing with Vashti, few people in the palace were calling the king's bluff or doubting he'd make drastic moves if necessary.

What also made Esther's situation particularly risky was the fact that the king had not invited her to see him in 30 days. Can you imagine not seeing your husband or wife for a month, just because you haven't received an invitation? Even so, after three days of fasting and praying, Esther woke up and prepared herself for her big day. She asked the Lord to soften her husband's heart, that he be receptive to seeing her and to accept her boldness in approaching him without an invitation.

As Esther put on her gown, she remembered that it was the king's favorite. She pulled back her hair in a matching ribbon and set off for the king's quarters. A hush fell on the servants as they watched her walk down the hall. The atmosphere was somber and the air was thick with anticipation. Somehow time seemed to stop as Esther took the long walk to the king's side of the palace. Each step was heavy with the weight of uncertainty, and her heart seemed to do a wild tap dance in her chest. Finally she reached the heavy curtains that separated her from the king. Before entering, she sent up a silent prayer. He heard the noise before he saw her and raised his voice: "Who's there!" The king was not expecting anyone to enter his quarters. Who would dare come uninvited? Didn't they know they could be killed for such an offense?

As the figure approached he began to make out who it was. Immediately, without knowing why, the king's heart began to melt. Although he hadn't necessarily wanted to see her before, suddenly the only person he wanted to be with was her.

"What a pleasant and very unexpected surprise, Esther." He immediately extended his beautifully decorated scepter. At that moment Esther's heart was as light as a feather; it was as though an enormous bag of bricks had been lifted from her. In the very least she would remain alive for the next few moments. Now she must explain the situation to her husband.

Esther obviously saw God from the MacGyver perspective. She took all of the necessary steps to involve God in her decision-making process, realized the seriousness of the situation, and brought people together to fast and pray. After hearing the problem, Esther knew what had to be done. Although we are given only a few verses of insight into the situation, we do not see Esther wavering or wallowing in a pool of indecision. It is evident that Esther knew she had been placed in this situation to help bring deliverance to her people. So she took action and by faith had the courage to take the risk of going in to the king and pleading for the deliverance of her people. To learn how this story ends, I invite you to continue by reading the book of Esther in the Bible.

If I compare the way Esther handled this situation and the way I handle my situations, I see that I often let timidity rule my life. But there's nothing timid about Esther in this story. In fact, an overly timid attitude is not a Godly characteristic. Second Timothy 1:7 says, "For God has not given us a spirit of fear, but of power and of love and of a sound mind" (NKJV).

This woman, who in the beginning of the story is known for her beauty, is later known for boldness. If I were Esther and continued my understanding of God as my "Superman" God, I would have expected God to intervene in a supernatural way without any involvement on my part. I would have never thought that God expected me to participate in the answer to my prayer by approaching the king to ask for mercy. But Esther had the courage to step out in faith and take a risk.

We often hear of risk when we speak of insurance or adventure sports, such as skydiving and bungee jumping, but risk is not limited to these areas. It's a real part of our lives. There are few certainties in this world (beside God and death). Everything else involves a risk. Just to clarify, I am not encouraging everyone to take unnecessary risks or to put your life in danger for the sake of taking a risk. What I *am* saying is that we must be willing to take risks within our Christian walk. Risk is allowing yourself to be placed in an uncomfortable position without knowing what the outcome might be. Do you think that Noah was comfortable as he preached of an onslaught of rain for 120 years before a single drop actually appeared? I would guess not, but it was the task that God gave him to do. And he had the courage to take the risk and do it.

Sometimes we have to take the jump, as in skydiving—it has to happen right before you're flying in the sky. If you stay where you are in your spiritual life and simply continue to do what you've always done, you will remain as stagnant as a pool of muddy water and get bored and always get the same results.

So what is the big risk that God wants you to take for Him? Are you praying about how to proceed in a particular situation? Sometimes we are told by God to wait, and sometimes we must take the first step in the direction He has pointed us. And just like MacGyver, He will help us find the solution through the situation.

Are you afraid to take the risk of trusting God with the most important areas of your life? Have you confined Him to things that are safe, saying such things as "God, You take the job of protecting my house and family and providing food and shelter, and I'll take on my money, wife, kids, and job"?

I've always wanted God to show up in a superheroic sort of a way. I've wanted my change to be dramatic, with background music and sound effects. Perhaps that's why I tend to move ahead of God. Perhaps when He's directing, I feel the story moves too slowly for me. I wait impatiently for the action to unfold and for the plot to thicken. I sit in burning anticipation to see the characters revealed, until finally I can no longer stand the suspense. As a result, I yank the director's horn from His hands and begin to call "Action!" while quickly redirecting the script. There's no risk in that at all; that's as safe as it comes—or so I might think.

So often in America we define our Christianity by our political stance on key issues, such as gay marriage and abortion. But when Christ was on earth, He was a social worker, not a politician. He concerned Himself with those who were poor and sick and dying, both spiritually and physically. The biggest risk we can take is to model our lives after the life of Christ. The way He lived was so radically different from the way we live, and the risk in doing this is that we'll be noticeably different than others. However, in order to do this, we must first get to know Him and learn to trust Him.

After you have established a relationship with God, I would encourage you to take the risk of trusting God with your life, plans, and desires. Bring them all to God and ask His opinion. In fact, ask Him to give you *new* plans and desires if the ones you presently have are not in line with what He wants.

Then take the risk of sharing your faith with someone else. This may be one of the hardest risks you'll have to take. When you establish a personal relationship with God, you are able to spend time with Him in the privacy of your home. However, when you share Him with others, you are required to become vulnerable and face the risk of rejection. But remember, risk is defined by putting yourself in an uncomfortable position for a good reason. While in this case the risk may be rejection, remember that it does not mean failure. When sharing God with others, Jesus said, "If the world hates you, keep in mind that it hated me first" (John 15:18).

Above all else, remember that it takes faith to have the courage to take risks for God. Even the risk of committing to the journey with God takes faith. But remember: "Without faith it is impossible to please Him, for he who comes to God must believe that He is, and that He is a rewarder of those who diligently seek Him" (Hebrews 11:6, NKJV).

Committing to the Journey

Learning How to Stick It Out
for the Long Haul:
The Stories of Saul and Joseph

Have you ever witnessed a love that has weathered the storm? Unfortunately, many of us in Generation X, Generation MTV, and Generation Y have seen our parents' marriages fall apart. We've seen the foundational institution that is supposed to stand the test of time crumble. For this reason it's hard for us to truly understand the concept of commitment. We're an instant-gratification generation, used to getting what we want right away, so we fail to understand that commitment is the wanting of what you have, even after you get it. We don't grasp the concept that commitment is about keeping your eyes fixed on the journey, and not spending all your time and focus on one-time events that take place along the way.

This failing is fueled by our society, which seems to be enthralled with weddings and cheating, both extraordinary and drama-filled experiences in a relationship. Networks boast strong ratings with shows that focus on the wedding day, the wedding-dress-buying, the stressed and crazed bride-to-be, and the scandalous extracurricular activities in which too many spouses find themselves involved. In focusing too much on these extraordinary events, we miss out on the experience of the journey. The same is often true in our relationship with Christ. While falling in love with Jesus is an important and amazing experience, there is still more to do to keep the fire alive. As we learned from the stories in the Bible, the characters mentioned not only have extraordinary experiences—they were also committed to pressing forward in their journeys with Christ.

For example, Saul had the extraordinary experience of being blinded on the road to Damascus on his way to persecute the Christians. During his journey he heard the voice of God ask him, "Saul, Saul, why do you persecute me?" (Acts 9:4). In this case, blindness was Saul's fish-food experience that led him to fall in love with Jesus. However, the story does not end there. Saul was baptized, and with his shift in his mission also came a new name—he was christened as Paul. And while the beginning of the story was extraordinary, it was the journey that really defined Paul's Christian life.

Similarly, Joseph's fish-food experience (Genesis 37; 39-45) had him thrown into a pit, sold into slavery, and carried far away from his home and family to Egypt. And while this is indeed an extraordinary set of events, throughout the journey we witness Joseph maturing and living out the values he was taught at home. During his journey he found himself working as Potiphar's servant, in charge of all the other servants, and then being accused of sexually assaulting Potiphar's wife. This accusation landed him in the slammer, where he met the pharaoh's baker and butler. From there God gave him the ability to interpret dreams, which would become his ticket to making it out of prison, and eventually catapulted him to become second to the pharaoh himself. Joseph could have easily gotten stuck on his one-time experience, but his commitment to riding out his journey with God led to him to live a life that was far more extraordinary than he could have possibly imagined.

While it's easy to focus on the current one-time big experience in your life (whether bad or good), you will see that God is in it for the long haul. So now that you've read through this book about relationship restoration with God, and learned about biblical characters who have often struggled in ways similar to your own struggles, you must answer the question: What is your "fish food" experience? What experience in your life seemed as though it would take you out, but instead God turned it around and used it to carry you through? What did it mean to your experience and your struggle? Did it cause you to make a commitment? Remember that as soon as you decide to take the first step with Jesus, you have embarked upon an exhilarating journey in your relationship with Him.

However, remember also that relationships have stages of maturity and, if the relationship is not nurtured, stages of degeneration as well. At the beginning the love is new and exciting. You hang on the person's every word and action. You're eager to know what they'll say or do or how they'll react in certain situations. However, as time progresses, the new car smell wears off and the love no longer feels new. If we're not careful, the same thing will happen in our relationship with God.

I would like to share some practical tips that can help you (and me) maintain a quality relationship with God. Some of these concepts you may recognize from chapter 7, but here is a consolidated reference list:

1. **Focus on relationship building.** Make a commitment to developing your relationship with God. Let Him know you intimately, and prepare to get to know Him intimately as well.

2. **Give God special time each day.** Set aside a special time each day for God. It works well for me to spend time with God in the morning. This way it helps me focus on what's truly important and put everything else into perspective for the day.

3. **Develop a prayer life.** Make prayer an important and nonnegotiable part of your life. Continuously keep the lines of communication open with God so that you can talk to Him and so that He can talk to you (1 Thessalonians 5:17).

4. **Study your Bible daily.** Many people discuss what the Bible says without ever opening it. Reading the Bible will give you insight on the struggles that many Bible characters went through. When I'm faced with a problem in life, I often try to think of a Bible character that went through something similar, then I compare the way I'm dealing with the situation with the way they dealt with it. Try reading along with an audio Bible. I've mentioned *Bible Experience* in this book because it has had a positive impact on my life, but you can use a number of others. I recommend that you start with the Gospels, Matthew, Mark, Luke, and John. Get to the heart of the matter and read about the life of Christ.

5. **Do something for God.** We often become uninterested in our human relationships when we no longer participate in them. The same is true in our relationship with God. You have to keep the relationship active. "Truly, I tell you, whatever you did for one of the least of these . . . you did for me" (Matthew 25:40). So if you are consistently forgetting to reach out to the world around you, you are not reaching out to God. Christianity is a contact sport—you can't be a benchwarmer Christian.

6. **Watch your appetite.** This doesn't mean to physically watch what you eat (though this is important as well); it means to be wary of what you take in. If you spend the entire day watching the *Real World Marathon* on MTV, it's unlikely that you'll have the desire to spend time with God directly afterward. If you eat apple-flavored candy before eating an apple, the apple is less likely to taste as sweet. The same is true in your spiritual life. The music, books, TV, and Internet you are consuming can dull your appetite for God.

7. **Join a church and get involved.** Another way that you can do something special for God is by getting involved in a church ministry. It's always great to have a church family that cares about you and that holds you accountable. It's also a great place to discover and use your spiritual gifts.

8. **Climb over spiritual brick walls.** For example, when a spiritual leader falls, you find out something unbelievable about a Christian friend, you find that people in church don't do what they say, or you find yourself bored in your relationship with God. These are walls we must climb over (with God's help). Previously when I hit spiritual brick walls, I would walk away from my relationship with God, because I didn't know how to deal with them. But instead of running into the brick wall, fight your way over it. This is part of the growth process. It's the same concept you face when working out. You will eventually plateau, and at this point you must address the problem and adjust your workout plan in order to keep growing. You must increase the weight or increase the reps. The same is true in our spiritual lives. We can't stay in the same spiritual spot all of our lives. Realize that people make mistakes and fall. Be forgiving and move forward. Get involved at church. Read a book of the Bible that you haven't read before. Tell your testimony, or what I like to call your "battle story." How has God worked in your life? Share it with those around you. Ask God to help you fight through the spiritual brick wall and to take you to the next level in your relationship with Him.

9. **Learn to follow God's will.** Learning to follow God's will is like a football game. At the beginning of the game you don't know you will win. You go in with a strategy, coaches, and players, but you don't know

when you will execute the plays, because you have not yet played this particular game against this particular opponent. But just because you don't know yet doesn't mean you quit the game halfway through. If the game's not going right, you listen to the coach, revise the strategy, and go back out to play. Your spiritual life is the same. Don't throw in the towel at halftime. Keep playing; keep seeking God's will. Take it play by play until you make it down the field.

Truly learning to stick it out for the long haul is really about discerning God's will for your life and learning to follow it. The phrase "discerning God's will" often carries a lot of mystery. What does it mean to discern God's will for your life? There have been several times in my life that I have truly tried to understand God's will. One particular instance was my asking God what I should do the summer before my last year of college. When I mentioned my dilemma to a friend, he recommended I read Morris Venden's book *How to Know God's Will in Your Life*. Because he was someone I trusted, I followed through on his advice and got the book. In it Venden outlined a helpful process for discerning God's will.

Decision time was approaching. The previous two summers I had interned at a large bank, and while I thoroughly benefited from the experience, I was also still young and had an adventurous attitude. I wanted to try something new. Then I found the perfect (or so I thought) opportunity. During a career fair at school I met a representative from a large state university who headed up a program that focused on international development. Everything about the position looked ideal. It offered an opportunity for a bilingual person to work in a developing country for the summer with pay.

I didn't see any reason I wouldn't get the position. Normally in these situations you don't know who your competition is. But in this case one of my classmates also applied. After a few weeks we were both called for phone interviews. Then we had to wait. I waited and waited until I got an envelope . . . but it wasn't a fat envelope. I guess you don't need a lot of space to extend a "thanks but no thanks." After receiving the news, I conferred with my classmate, only to learn that he *did* receive the position. While I was happy for him and felt he deserved it, I couldn't help feeling a tinge of disappointment. The situation left me thoroughly confused about what God wanted from me.

A few days later the group with which I studied abroad in Spain a year earlier was visiting campus to make a presentation and promote the program. One of my friends asked if I would come and share my experience with the group. I was more than happy to do so. After making my presentation, I listened to the director of the program talk about the countries that were available for study abroad. One really stuck out in my mind: Brazil. Initially I thought, *I can't go study abroad again. I've already had that experience.* But somehow the nagging wouldn't go away, until I finally realized that's what I should be doing that summer. As you read in chapter 1, it was there that I had an amazing experience with God; I was able to see people who had genuine relationships with Him, and I made some great friends. Although I didn't get what I initially wanted, God gave me a different experience that exceeded my expectations.

This is the gist of following God's will for your life. Proceeding in life step by step, following what you know and can see right now. It's about hanging on.

One day as I was driving home, I witnessed a small piece of nature. Being surrounded by a forest of glass and steel buildings, I seldom encounter nature. So you can imagine my delight (or rather a chill of fear down my spine) when I saw a small brown spider perched on top of the side view mirror of my car. At the time I was securely tucked into the driver's seat of my car, prepared to drive off. And though the spider was less than an inch wide, I was just as distracted as I would have been had an elephant plopped into the passenger's seat. I took off slowly and glanced over periodically, mostly out of curiosity. Then I began to pick up speed, watching if the force of the wind would knock it off my car.

As I pulled to a stoplight, I glanced over in surprise to see the eight-legged creature firmly planted where I first saw it. So as soon as I got to the green light I floored the gas pedal. The spider seemed to disappear, though later I learned that it had cleverly lowered itself from the top of the side view mirror into the cup of the mirror to shield itself from the force of the wind. When I pulled into my driveway, the spider smugly returned to the original position on top of the mirror, looking a bit triumphant. Although I dislike spiders, I must admit that I learned a lesson from that one. Clamp down. Hold one. Hide yourself in God in the hard times. Make a commitment and mean the words you say. Don't focus on the one-time events in your relationship with God. Focus on the day-to-day. Focus on the journey.

Are God and Christianity relevant in the world today? Are the ideas in the Bible outdated or old-fashioned? Are the principles in the Bible sluggish at best in trying to keep up with our ever-evolving world? Does the Bible promote intolerance of other religions and people who straddle the gender lines? There are those who doubt that the Bible is a timeless book of wisdom. After all, how could those authors write something that would be relevant today? They could not know how technology would evolve and the issues with which we'd have to grapple would come about. So is our God and our Christianity prepared to deal with this? From personal experience I can say that the Bible *is* relevant. A read of the Gospels will reveal a Jesus you may not have expected. The principles He taught *are* timeless. They're not always popular or easy, and for this reason people say they are out of date, but they are indeed relevant. His interactions with people show that He is more tolerant than anyone you've ever met. The theme of the Bible is love, and Jesus showed that in every interaction He had. So what's holding you back from making a commitment today?

Is it your fear? "For the Spirit God gave us does not make us timid, but gives us power, love and self-discipline (2 Timothy 1:7).

Is it your family? "Though my father and mother forsake me, the Lord will receive me" (Psalm 27:10).

Is it your inability? "I can do all this through him who gives me strength" (Philippians 4:13).

Are you scared that you won't have what you need? "And my God will meet all your needs according to the riches of his glory in Christ Jesus" (Philippians 4:19).

Are you scared about the future? "My Father's house has many rooms; if it were not so, would I have told you that. I am going there to prepare a place for you? And if I go and prepare a place for you, I will come back and take you to be with me that you also may be where I am" (John 14:2, 3).

Do you think you'll miss out on something? "However, as it is written: 'What no eye has seen, what no ear has heard, and what no human has conceived'—the things God has prepared for those who love him—these are the things God has revealed to us by his Spirit" (1 Corinthians 2:9).

Are you worried you won't enjoy the Sabbath? "Then he said to them, 'The Sabbath was made for man, not man for the Sabbath'" (Mark 2:27).

Are you scared that God doesn't know the best plan for your life? "'For I know the plans I have for you,' declares the Lord, 'plans to prosper you and not to harm you, plans to give you hope and a future'" (Jeremiah 29:11).

Be prepared, willing, and open for the journey. Make a commitment today.